CHIP BUGNAR

GRACE
BEYOND THE VEIL:
The Mystery in Ephesians

ISBN: 0692358625
ISBN 13: 9780692358627

CONTENTS

PREFACE

MY HOPE FOR THIS BOOK is that the church will be able to plumb a little deeper into the incalculable riches of Jesus Christ through Paul's short letter to the Ephesians. I pray alongside Paul's prayer for the original recipients of this letter that the Spirit of revelation would peel back the curtain so that we may see God for who He is. Beholding God as He truly is transforms people. It certainly has me.

This book zooms in and out on Ephesians, in hopes of helping you sense the big picture while we also dive into the details. The "mystery" - God's "mystery" - sets the stage for how we will look at Ephesians together. The first section traces this thread under the heading "The Mystery Unveiled." The second section follows Paul's change of tone in Chapters 4-6 of Ephesians through the lens of "The Mystery Unleashed."

There is no shortage of literature on the mystery in Ephesians. I am indebted to many of those works. What do I hope this book adds to the discussion? This book represents my attempt to unpack the mystery in a way that remains tethered to the context of Ephesians. If Paul merely wanted us to understand God's mystery, he would have concluded his letter at the end of chapter 3. But three chapters remain. Why? Because the mystery mandates a new mission. Ephesians opens up a new world of God's activity and grace to us, where He is at work restoring what is broken through Jesus Christ. This new world demands a new walk.

I firmly believe that if God opens our eyes to His mystery, we will not remain the same. We simply can't. His plan is just too big to be left on the sidelines. The mystery's unveiling awakens us. It beckons us. It unleashes us into the world that has yet to be clued in.

I hope you will read this book in one hand while holding Ephesians in the other. I have chosen the Holman Christian Standard Bible translation for its faithfulness to capture the original intent of Paul in a readable and accessible flow.

Special thanks to my wife, Bec, whose countless sacrifices to make a project like this a reality have not gone unnoticed. The fact that I get the privilege of doing life with you never ceases to amaze me. Becky and George, thank you for raising such a godly daughter. And to my kids, your joy with me in this project has been such an encouragement. James, Jennifer, Daniel, Ed, Nick, and Pri - thank you for your help with different facets of this book. And for those saints who have helped me understand and apply the gospel through deep community - Dave, Daniel, Pri, Seth, Ben, David, Sean, Andy, Ed, Mark, and Andrew – I am thankful for each one of you. I also want to thank my Dad and Mom, whose beautiful marriage points beyond their own.

INTRODUCTION

WHEN WE STARTED THE JOURNEY of moving to Central Asia we had no idea all that would be involved. Moving overseas takes a certain kind of person. My wife handled it beautifully. She loathes hoarding so it became a good excuse to narrow in on what we really enjoy and what we actually use. Six people travelling with sixteen bags has a way of sifting through the stuff that just accumulates over time. Needless to say, the yard sale a few weeks before we left had some gems for cheap.

The few things that survived the judgment - the few that she actually kept - she treasured. One of them was a plate that her college roommate, Robin, had painted as a gift for our wedding. It had the words of Joshua 24:15, "As for me and my house, we will serve the Lord," around the edge of it. That plate reminded her of Robin, of us, and our calling. It reminded us of our resolve as a family to "serve the Lord." And as a painting, it captured my wife's colors and style perfectly. It was her story. It was her. We carefully packed it, wrapping it with bubble wrap, and surrounded it with clothes. It had to survive the journey.

But the journey proved too much. (Just what happens down those conveyor belts?) Thankfully, our dear friend, Julie, who helped us navigate the journey to Turkey and unpacked most of our stuff, saw the broken plate first. She gathered the pieces and quietly tucked it away in her bag. Bec remained in the dark. Julie knew the stress of leaving family and moving overseas did not need another downer.

After Julie finished helping set up our house during the day, she stayed the night with some friends of ours. When she arrived at their house, she began working. Her super glue in hand, she took what was left of the plate and pieced it all back together. A few days later, right before she returned to America, her repairs were done. She craftily snuck the plate in to our apartment and placed it on top of the refrigerator as if it had been there the whole time. When Bec found it, she didn't even realize it had been broken. It was not until a few days later that Julie let her in on the secret.

Julie had restored what the journey had broken. Bec had no clue. In the midst of all the transition and her world that had been turned upside down, a restoration effort was underway.

The journey of life proves too much for us as well. We may not even realize the extent of the damage. But what if there is more to the story? What if there was hope for the brokenness? What if there is a "Julie," who behind the scenes, is at work piecing it all together? What if the shattered pieces, may be without us even realizing it, were being picked up by the One who had the power to mend them?

We are introduced to just such a Being in the book of Ephesians. That is the God revealed in this six-chapter letter that was written about 2,000 years ago. In generations past, He tucked away the details of His plan but now has let us in on His secret. The news is out. He is restoring what is broken through Jesus Christ. Paul labels that act of mending the "mystery" in Ephesians. God gathers the pieces. God knows how every single one fits back together. His hands gently restore what is broken. And He has not left us in the dark. He has let His secret out.

There is more to our stories than the brokenness we see and feel. The knowledge itself induces a certain degree of hope. But to see it unfolding before our very eyes – that would change everything. A whole new world would open before us. That new world awaits everyone who opens the book of Ephesians.

CHAPTER 1

A Song of Love Unknown

Ephesians 1:3-14

THE YEAR WAS 1983. That is when the miracle upset occurred. College basketball witnessed its own David take down Goliath on a last second dunk which crowned NC State the victor over star-studded Houston. Maybe you remember the shot from near half-court. Maybe you remember the dunk. Whatever you may remember, one thing remains etched in your mind after seeing that moment: Coach Valvano's mad scramble across the court in absolute joy. The childlike amazement written on his face captured the wonder, the surprise, the relief, the pride, the miracle. The underdog, against all odds, had overcome.

The opening chapter of Ephesians brings us to another man in a similar state of elated joy. He had been made the unlikely recipient of an inheritance that promised unending joy. This man was the Apostle Paul. We do not need to see his face because his pen is let loose, scrambling to find the words. The surprise, the wonder, the relief of the grace of God sends Paul's pen running back and forth with praise after praise. It makes one wonder - when the believers at Ephesus gathered in someone's home to read this letter to the community, just how did they capture all the emotion and gratitude of this first chapter? What tone is appropriate? Singing seems more fitting than simply reading it aloud. The apostle simply overwhelms us because he was overwhelmed. One thanksgiving gives way to another from verse 3 all the way to 14. It comes at you like an avalanche of praise. Watch the momentum and mass keep building as we read Ephesians 1:3-14:

> "Praise the God and Father of our Lord Jesus Christ, who has blessed us in Christ with every spiritual blessing in the heavens. For He chose us in Him, before the foundation of the world, to be holy and blameless in His sight. In love He predestined us to be adopted through Jesus Christ for Himself, according to His favor and will, to the praise of His glorious grace that He favored us with in the Beloved.
>
> We have redemption in Him through His blood, the forgiveness of our trespasses, according to the riches of His grace that He lavished on us with all wisdom and understanding. He made known to us the mystery of His will, according to His good pleasure that He planned in Him for the administration of the days of fulfillment — to bring everything together in the Messiah, both things in heaven and things on earth in Him.
>
> We have also received an inheritance in Him, predestined according to the purpose of the One who works out everything in agreement with the decision of His will, so that we who had already put our hope in the Messiah might bring praise to His glory.
>
> When you heard the message of truth, the gospel of your salvation, and when you believed in Him, you were also sealed with the promised Holy Spirit. He is the down payment of our inheritance, for the redemption of the possession, to the praise of His glory."

Paul's heart simply could not contain what God had set in motion in Christ. Nothing compared with the glory of God's love in Christ. It stretched imagination. It challenged his categories. His song was love unknown.[1]

Paul wanted the believers in Asia Minor to join his song. That is why he unpacks the riches of God's grace. In these 11 verses, verses 3-14, we overhear Paul praising God for one glorious act after another. May God give us ears to hear this song as well as the grace to join it as we consider the content together.

In this set of verses, did you notice that Paul repeats himself over and over? He cannot seem to move beyond something. Or I should say Someone. It is Jesus. Jesus Christ occupies center stage in God's redemptive drama. He is at the center of all that God has done, is doing, and will do. The spotlight never shifts away from Christ. All spiritual blessings are tethered to Him. Redemption is "in Him." Believers are chosen "in Him." Adoption is "through Jesus Christ." Grace is found "in Him." Everything comes together "in the Messiah." This concept of being "in Christ" and every blessing from God flowing "through Christ" reappears 13 times in the original Greek language. It is Christ who holds the key that unlocks God's richest treasures. Paul's redundancy stems from Christ's supremacy.

There is a refrain to Paul's "song" that reveals God's intentions through Christ. The core of this refrain repeats itself three times in these verses. What is the end goal of God's redemptive story? Paul makes it clear (emphasis mine):

- "He predestined us to be adopted through Jesus Christ for Himself, according to His favor and will, *to the praise of His glorious grace* that He favored us with in the Beloved." (1:5-6)

---

[1] "My Song Is Love Unknown," a hymn written by Samuel Crossman, 1664.

3

- ". . . so that we who had already put our hope in the Messiah might bring *praise to His glory.*"(1:12)

- "He is the down payment of our inheritance, for the redemption of the possession, to the *praise of His glory.*" (1:14)

Praise is the goal, redemption the means. God is out to so overwhelm us in Christ that praise is the only fitting response. This is God's purpose in sharing His Beloved Son with us. All glory echoes back to Him. Praise is the culmination of His initiative toward us. Praise is the hug at half-court when Coach Valvano's joy was made complete. In Ephesians 1, God chooses and creates a choir - a holy and blameless people who reflect His glory and sing His praise. It is their praise that completes His purpose.

In a reflex compelled by God's lavish grace, Paul's heart blesses this God who had blessed him in Ephesians 1:3-14. This isn't the rehearsing of facts from a theological treatise. His heart overflows in grateful praise. This is what happens when God's grace grips the heart. People start singing because they can't help it. Grace streams in and songs flow out.

The gracious disposition of God toward us will never change and never be exhausted. He loves to be gracious toward us in Christ. This God, out of His freedom and unconstrained favor, chooses us - unworthy as we are - to be the objects of His grace. God simply sets His love upon us when as sinners we deserve judgment. He chooses to include us when we deserve eternal exclusion. Grace came to us. Grace laid claim on us. Apart from anything in ourselves, unlikely recipients as we may be, recipients we are. We find ourselves enveloped in this triune expression of love and unity. The Father, Son, and Spirit are actively showering us with grace and securing our eternal inheritance. Paul was floored. It's what grace does. It leaves us lost in wonder.

Part of what amazes us about grace is how freely it comes to us. A gift so great awakens in us this impulse to pay for it in some way, to lay some claim upon it with our own merit or worth. It is too much indebtedness to handle. We cannot just accept this, can we? "Let's split the cost," we reason to ourselves. But we look around and there is nothing we can bring to the table. Everything we brought to the table should have excluded us but somehow, in a surprise of grace, we get in by no merit of our own.

Our humility deepens as we reread verses 3-14 and realize that the cost of our inclusion has been paid by Someone else. This free grace toward us cost Jesus everything: "We have redemption in Him through His blood, the forgiveness of our trespasses, according to the riches of His grace" (Ephesians 1:7). The word "blood" expresses this price so succinctly that it is easy to pass it over. The agony, the anguish, the struggle, the hurt, the wrath, the hostility, the pain, the forsakenness, the loneliness, the injustice are all captured in that one word with horrific simplicity. He died for us on that tree. He did it all. It is finished. This fact just furthers our praise as we realize God's initiative toward us came with a great cost. This bloody price has a double effect upon us: it wins us to God and woos us to God. It issues forth redemption and praise. Paul writes, "In love He predestined us to be adopted through Jesus Christ for Himself" (Ephesians 1:5). There is no other place we'd rather be.

These gracious surprises never stop so the song never ends. God included us "so that in the coming ages He [God] might display the immeasurable riches of His grace through His kindness to us in Christ Jesus" (Ephesians 2:7). God isn't finished. Every new dimension of glory of the coming ages flows to us from grace and through grace and so that we might experience more grace. Grace covers past guilt, supplies present faith, and awaits us in future glory. The endless age to come can never dry the infinite well of God's grace in Christ. Ten thousand days won't take the sweetness from God's grace. It will be just as fresh then as it was to Paul in Ephesians 1.

This glorious future isn't merely a possibility for the redeemed. It's a reality. This never-ending grace already envelops us in Christ. We are sealed for our future inheritance through the Spirit God imparted to us. The Holy Spirit reserves God's riches for us and preserves us for God's riches. Through Him, we have a taste of what is to come. The future has entered the present. Paul calls this initial experience of glory a "down payment" of the inheritance (1:14). The Spirit's presence assures us of God's love and secures our eternal enjoyment of it. He ushers us to glory.

Paul's song has begun. Has yours? Those who are in Christ resonate with Paul's joy in Chapter 1. Are you in Christ? The Ephesian believers were made partakers of this glory when they "heard the message of truth" and believed in Jesus. Paul further describes the "message of truth" as the "the gospel of your salvation" (1:13). The way to join the song is through simply hearing the good news and believing in its goodness for you. This belief is a posture of relinquishing our efforts of self-salvation and resting in the only way God has provided to be saved: in Jesus. His blood sufficiently covers all our sin. His resurrection proves it. I opened this chapter by saying all of God's blessings are tethered to Jesus. The way we are tethered to Jesus is through the Spirit that comes through faith in Him.

For those who are in Christ, the glory of Ephesians 1:3-14 has yet to be fully discovered. There are still unknown realms of endless love before us.

"My song is love unknown,
My Savior's love to me;
Love to the loveless shown,
That they might lovely be.

O who am I,
That for my sake
My Lord should take
Frail flesh and die?"[2]

---

[2] "My Song Is Love Unknown," a hymn written by Samuel Crossman, 1664.

Part 1: The Mystery Unveiled

CHAPTER 2

Spoiler Alert

Ephesians 1:9-11

He God made known to us the *mystery* of His will, according to His good pleasure that He planned in Him for the administration of the days of fulfillment — to bring everything together in the Messiah, both things in heaven and things on earth in Him.

— Ephesians 1:9-11

P AUL'S PRAISE IN EPHESIANS 1 doesn't merely unpack God's redemptive work in Christ but peels back the curtain on all of human history. We get a behind-the-scenes look at why the world was made and where the world is headed. Ephesians 1:9-11 gives the conclusion. It's the epic spoiler alert that doesn't leave you disinterested in the movie but leaves you even more anxious to see it. It's the dramatic conclusion that enlarges the pleasure of the present, not vice-versa. These three verses thrill the imagination with pregnant anticipation of what life will be like when God's program is complete. "Both things in heaven and things on earth" are coming together in Jesus (1:9-11). Just what will that moment entail?

This never-ending conclusion when redemption spills over into creation Paul describes as "the mystery of His [God's] will" (Ephesians 1:9a). God Himself has now stepped in to unveil the closing act to which history hastens. He has let humanity in on the mystery, the final outworking of His plan. God is tying up all the loose ends in Jesus. This moment that brings purpose and meaning to everything, this day when hope gives way to sight – that's the mystery's apex.

We learn here in verses 9-11 that the mystery is God's script for the story that drives the human drama to that glorious consummation. The world began for Christ. The world will end at Christ's feet. This is the story He scripted for creation. From Christ, through Christ, and for Christ captures the heart of what God's will is. The mystery presses history toward that climax of joy and peace when Christ's fullness fills the heavens and the earth.

This means that God ushers the world's brokenness toward unity in the Messiah, Jesus Christ. It means that there is hope. It's no secret that the world isn't right. The horrors of war, the tragedies of deadly viruses, the hollowness of our own stories reinforce the one universally held truth: something is off. Just by the looks of things, it seems like the drama in which we find ourselves is meaningless and moves forward with no real purpose. No overarching goal.

But that's just on the surface. Underneath the pain, behind the scenes, the mystery of God's will is unfolding. That's what God has unveiled in Ephesians. By God's good pleasure and administrative wisdom, human history is being guided toward this glorious consummation. In Christ, heaven and earth will reunite in perfect wholeness and delight.

This "mystery" forms the lens through which I want to explore the meaning of Ephesians alongside you. It's not a mystery in the way we might think. It isn't mystical, doesn't deal with fantasy, and isn't unclear. The word "secret" falls so short. "Mystery," as Paul uses it, is something that was revealed in part in the past but now has been made known with more specificity and clarity than previous generations imagined. God has clued us in to His plan for the world. A plan that, despite the looks of things, brings everything together in Jesus. This is good news!

Paul opens Ephesians with the spoiler. The mystery's ending opens our eyes to the big picture of Ephesians and to our place in the story. This conclusion means "on earth as it is in heaven" (Matthew 6:10b) will no longer be the longing of faith. It will no longer dwell in the unseen. It will work itself out in reality. Heaven comes home to earth. God's kingdom sets everything right. Christ's fullness overwhelms. That knowledge sends Paul soaring in Chapter 1 and to the nations in Chapter 3 of Ephesians. This mystery must get out. The vision of the mystery - formerly hidden and now unveiled - transforms Paul's own vision for his life, for the church, and for the world.

If we see it, through this six-chapter letter written 2,000 years ago, we will be transformed as well.

A Bird's Eye View of the Mystery

Since the mystery forms the lens through which we will explore Ephesians, let's look carefully together at all the references to the word "mystery" in the book of Ephesians (emphasis mine):

> "He [God] made known to us the **mystery** of His will, according to His good pleasure that He planned in Him for the administration of the days of fulfillment —to bring everything together in the Messiah, both things in heaven and things on earth in Him" (Ephesians 1:9-11).

"The *mystery* was made known to me by revelation, as I have briefly written above. By reading this you are able to understand my insight about the *mystery* of the Messiah. This was not made known to people in other generations as it is now revealed to His holy apostles and prophets by the Spirit: The Gentiles are coheirs, members of the same body, and partners of the promise in Christ Jesus through the gospel. I was made a servant of this gospel by the gift of God's grace that was given to me by the working of His power" (Ephesians 3:3-7).

"This grace was given to me—the least of all the saints—to proclaim to the Gentiles the incalculable riches of the Messiah, and to shed light for all about the administration of the *mystery* hidden for ages in God who created all things. This is so God's multi-faceted wisdom may now be made known through the church to the rulers and authorities in the heavens" (Ephesians 3:8-10).

"For this reason a man will leave his father and mother and be joined to his wife, and the two will become one flesh. This *mystery* is profound, but I am talking about Christ and the church" (Ephesians 5:32).

"Pray also for me, that the message may be given to me when I open my mouth to make known with boldness the *mystery* of the gospel" (Ephesians 6:19).

This book traces the mystery through two governing headings. "The Mystery Unveiled" explains Ephesians 1-3 where Paul focuses primarily on the content of the mystery. "The Mystery Unleashed" governs Chapters 4-6 of Ephesians where Paul unpacks how the mystery transforms the new community that displays its power, the church. The first three chapters of Ephesians focus on God's activity and the last three on our response to His initiative.

Our time in Chapters 1-3 of Ephesians will be spent zooming out and seeing the world in a new way as God has let us peek into His design. This won't move verse by verse, whereas the section unpacking Chapters 4-6 will move more section-by-section, verse-by-verse. As we consider these chapters together, we will focus on the implications for our churches as we are transformed by this mystery.

• • •

The World Gone Wrong: A Cosmic Divorce

The mystery's completion promises that heaven will reunite with earth in Jesus. To understand why that is such good news, we need to dig a little deeper. Just what is it about this world that needs God's mystery? What has gone wrong that needs to be made right?

To understand the cosmic division that must be overcome, we have to go back to the beginning. Adam and Eve were created and given a secure home in the garden of Eden. This idyllic garden is portrayed in Genesis and by the prophets as a kind of portal where heaven met earth in perfect fullness (Ezekiel 28:13-14). God and man dwelled together. Everything was in order. God ruled man. Man and woman ruled the earth. The earth, being made for them, submitted to their rule. It was "very good" (Genesis 1:31). The man and woman lived off the infinite resourcefulness of this self-replenishing garden. They rested in God's perfect provision. This place was unlike any place we have ever encountered in our post-Genesis 3 world. This was life in the garden of Eden.

God designed the world to make sense. He interwove wholeness into the very fabric of the world He declared good. This sense of satisfaction, of "fit-ness," is wrapped up in God's seal of approval when He labeled creation "very good" and rested on the seventh day. The goodness of God spilled over into the goodness of creation for mankind in the beginning. Man was at rest in a world at rest.

The wholeness of Eden expressed itself through their oneness as a couple: "Both the man and his wife were naked, yet felt no shame" (Genesis 2:25). This isn't less than literal. It's gloriously more. They were naked. They were unashamed. But these signify so much more than mere physical and emotional states. Their marital fullness expressed the fullness that was Eden. Their togetherness perfectly expressed Eden's. The two were one in a place where heaven met earth as one.

Even though they had everything, Adam and Eve stopped listening to their good Creator's voice and turned to creation, reversing the order that God established. They imagined "rest" beyond their rest. They believed the lie that God was limiting them by forbidding the tree. In a quest for more, they ate from the tree of the knowledge of good and evil. That bite changed everything. That knowledge of evil proved much less satisfying than the serpent promised.

Feeling shame for the first time, they sought to cover themselves with the leaves from the very trees God had given them. This covering wasn't sufficient. They sensed God walking by, and for the first time, they felt the impulse to run and hide. Everything had changed. This ruptured relationship brought fear. Unity gave way to alienation. They felt the first empty cries of deficiency. Their previous unity was exchanged for distance and shame. Naked trust in one another gave way to finger-pointing and division. God's firm yet inviting words, "Where are you?" started the sorrowful exchange that exposed their guilt.

In a just exchange, God gave them what they sinfully craved. They chose creation over their Creator, so He let them go their own way. They soon discovered that having the world wasn't all it was cracked up to be. It wouldn't satisfy and wouldn't end well. The dust would swallow them in death. The former resourcefulness of Eden's delights was exchanged for the barrenness of thorns and thistles. Now, their own relationship would be marked by shame and strife. In one bitter bite, Adam and Eve chose earth over heaven. And earth they could have. God stationed two angels to guard the way to the tree of life, exiling them from Eden to wander the wilderness with only the memories of Eden. Sin's aftershocks were felt at every level. God and man, man and woman, man and the world, and even heaven and earth were ruptured that day. Sin gave birth to this divorce of cosmic proportions.

Sin has cast a dark shadow over every age and generation. It's why Eden seems so distant, so unimaginable. Our categories fail us. The effects of this divorce painfully linger today. Adam and Eve's shame resides in ours. Rest eludes us. Relational pain walls us in. Guilt sends us running for cover amid the trees. Some of us wish we could hide from ourselves and even become someone else. War saddens us. Cancer kills us. We're a mess. The world we live in is a mess. Just look at our scars. This place doesn't feel like home because it isn't.

My four children love the game Minecraft. This phenomenon of a game has them creating mini-worlds in which they live and build. These worlds stretch on and on. They design farmlands. They erect skyscraping hotels. They relive Disney by creating their own roller coasters. Their detailed imaginations amaze me as they take me on a tour through their worlds. One night at the dinner table, Emma was afraid to talk to Ben about what had happened earlier in his mini-world. Emma was digging around some lava in Ben's mountain house, when she fell into a hole and died. If you die in the game, they tell me, you can "regenerate" and you will reappear. There is just one huge problem. You don't regenerate in the same place. Emma ended up somewhere else in Ben's world and couldn't find her way back. Emma's death also meant the loss of Ben's home. That sounds a lot like how death works in Genesis 3. Sin put us farther from home than we realized and we have lost the way back.

The book of Ecclesiastes describes a man's attempt to rediscover man's true home, Eden. We hear in the Preacher's "confessions" the same painful hollowness that reverberates through our own journals and the daily headlines. We are lost. The Preacher's quest consistently leaves him empty-handed: "This too is futile and a pursuit of the wind" (Ecclesiastes 2:17, 3:23, 2:26, 3:4, 3:8, 4:16, 6:9, etc.) If anyone had a chance to find Eden again, he did. He had the resources to unearth heaven on earth. Work, wealth, women, wisdom, power - he had it all. But all of it, he declared, was "absolutely futile, everything is futile" (Ecclesiastes 12:8). That tragic stamp on his investigation reveals just how far we've come from God's stamp in Genesis 1 of "very good." This is why theologians have labeled the first sin "The Fall." Heaven has been barred from earth, and we're lost in the hole we dug for ourselves.

Author Cornelius Plantinga captures this rupturing of creation well when he wrote:

> "We must see the fall as anti-creation, the blurring of distinctions, and the rupturing of bonds, and the one as a result of the other. Thus, human beings who to be 'like God, knowing good and evil,' succeed only in alienating themselves from God and from each other. Even the good and fruitful earth becomes their foe. (Genesis 3:17-18, 4:12-14) . . . The story of the fall tells us that sin corrupts: it puts asunder what God had joined together and joins together what God had put asunder."[3]

Thankfully, there is more to the story.

---

[3] Cornelius Plantinga, *Not the Way It's Supposed to Be: A Breviary of Sin,* Wm. B. Eerdmans Publishing Co., 1995. pgs. 29-30.

The World Made Right: A Mystery-Made Reunion

If we search for answers merely through experience, we, like the Preacher, will keep searching and never find them. Our restlessness will remain. But Ephesians 1 takes us beyond experience to revelation. God has made known that His mystery will win over the mess. Looking merely "under the sun" leaves so many unanswered questions (Ecclesiastes 6:1). But Ephesians 1 broadens the horizon. God speaks from heaven, beyond the sun, to unveil the mystery. Heaven and earth will reunite in Christ; God has ordained this glorious reunion. In the mystery, God is ushering heaven down the aisle to re-embrace earth. He brings "everything together in the Messiah" . . . "For God was pleased to have all His fullness dwell in Him, and through Him to reconcile everything to Himself by making peace through the blood of His cross" (Ephesians 1:10; Colossians 1:19-20b). It's a mystery-made reunion.

The earth itself yearns for this reunion. It craves to be free of its inability to serve man with heaven's resourcefulness again, as it was in Eden. Creation groans under the oppressive weight of the curse. Romans 8 portrays creation kicking and screaming, refusing to settle into its subjection to futility. It longs for redemption and yearns to yield the bounty of Eden again: "For we know that the whole creation has been groaning together with labor pains until now" (Romans 8:22). The picture here is of creation being pregnant, suffering birth pains. Reading the mystery from Ephesians alongside Romans 8, it is the mystery that fuels this defiance to the curse. God's mystery guarantees these pains will produce life. Man will be set free from sin. Creation will be set free from futility. Christ's fullness will fill heaven and earth. These groanings will not end in vain. Divorce will not have the last word. It is no match for the mystery.

This moment will be the peak of human delight and fulfillment. Eden 2.0. God is not merely rewinding the script though. He is doing something new. This restoration effort, this reunification plan, is why the mystery in

Ephesians rekindles hope and awakens joy. Paradise lost will be paradise regained, and what is coming far outweighs what once was. The blessing will win over the curse. Everything, everywhere, at every moment is being funneled into one climactic crescendo at Jesus' feet.

A Huge Relief

This is good news because despite our desperate attempts, we cannot fix the world. It is not ours to fix. We are unable even to fix what is broken in our own lives. We are not the saviors of our own stories. God has mercifully taken this exhausting burden from us who are in Christ Jesus. We do not have to piece together the thousands of scattered experiences that shape our lives. God's mystery rescues us from solving the riddle which is us.

If our lives were bound in a book, nearly every page would reveal our brokenness. If we zoom out and include everyone's story, the scattered pieces become too overwhelming to even consider. My dad learned firsthand how picking up the pieces can be too much to handle a few years ago. He would regularly mow the lawn during his lunch break in his suit. The neighbors called it a "business cut." One day he was mowing the grass on his new John Deere with his wallet in his pocket. As he followed the edge between the already mown grass and the taller grass in the front lawn, before his reflexes could respond, his wallet slipped from his pocket, hit the ground beside the mower, and was sucked underneath into the blade. "Crunch!" It wasn't over yet. His lawnmower didn't have just one blade. It was a mulching blade that had many blades rotating in different directions. This "crunch" lasted a few seconds. He looked back and to the side to see the horror of thousands of pieces of credit cards, insurance cards, his driver's license, cash, and leather scattered all over the front lawn. The next few hours and days were spent combing the lawn, picking up the pieces, and trying to make some sense of it all. My mom and dad finally gave up because the task was just too large. There were too many pieces.

The world is like that mulching blade, chewing us up and scattering us all around. We are like my mom and dad - combing around looking for the piece that will fix our brokenness. Worry is one way we comb around, consumed by resolving the tension in our lives. Insecurity settles in because we have this lingering doubt that we won't be able to piece it back together. Fear and despair may settle in because life doesn't wait for us to repair it before more pain comes. Loss is loss. Life is too much of a mess.

But the God revealed in Ephesians 1 rescues us from this futile task. Entrusting our future into His able hands enables us to stop combing around the mess we've made. He is the Administrating Author, working everything for His good pleasure. God planned for Christ to be the glue that holds everything together. Our self-devised solutions cannot compare with His. God is tying the seemingly loose ends of the whole, grand narrative together, including the little narrative strands of our own lives. He will bring heaven to earth in Christ for the everlasting inheritance of the redeemed. He will leave no piece still scattered or lost: "We know that all things work together for the good of those who love God: those who are called according to His purpose" (Romans 8:28). That is the relief the mystery now revealed brings.

In Ephesians 1:13-14, Paul outlines how the believers at Ephesus were able to get in on this mystery-made reunion: "When you heard the message of truth, the gospel of your salvation, and when you believed in Him, you were also sealed with the promised Holy Spirit. He is the down payment of our inheritance, for the redemption of the possession, to the praise of His glory." It is the same today. The process has not changed. We have to put down our "combs" - our attempts to solve the puzzle. It is God who saves. God secures this future for those who hear the gospel and believe in Jesus. Hearing about Jesus and believing on Jesus rescues us from our futility. God assures those who are in Christ of their eternal inheritance by binding them to hope through the "promised Holy Spirit." This Spirit preserves those who believe until redemption reaches its consummation. This saving work is from beginning to end, start to finish - God's work through Christ, imparted to us by the Spirit.

A few years ago, my wife and I, like millions of others, became enthralled by the ABC series *Lost*. The story's oddness puzzled us, so we slavishly watched all 121 episodes, trying to figure it out. We were addicted. Six years into the series the time had finally come for the concluding episode. Our friends came over. We offered each other our best guesses as to what would happen. But then the final scene came. Dud. So much was left unanswered that we sent our friends home and went to bed completely frustrated. It was a huge bust. We were disgusted with ourselves - with the writers - with the world even! Six years of Wednesday nights wasted. The anticipated moment that promised resolution ended so empty. The narrative tangents that teased us were left dangling. Things didn't add up, and it seemed like the writers of the show were themselves "lost." In this way, the conclusion hit too close to home. It actually tasted too much like real life. It became a bitter echo of our culture's lostness.

Contrast that picture with the "mystery" that God superintends in Ephesians 1. He steers the story. He knows the beginning and the end. His hand guides the universe toward its satisfying resolution in Christ. He is not lost in the narrative. He stands over it, pressing it toward wholeness in Jesus. Like a master conductor, He takes each narrative strand and weaves it into the song. He wrote the plot and secures its resolution. His conclusion will not leave those in Christ hanging. The mystery must culminate in satisfying praise to the One who scripted it all.

William Cowper captured the restful posture of the redeemed in his hymn entitled "God Moves in a Mysterious Way"[4]:

---

[4] William Cowper, "God Moves in a Mysterious Way," in *Twenty-six Letters on Religious Subjects* by John Newton, 1774.

"God moves in a mysterious way,
His wonders to perform;
He plants His footsteps in the sea,
And rides upon the storm.

Deep in unfathomable mines,
Of never failing skill
He treasures up His bright designs
And works His sovereign will.
Ye fearful saints, fresh courage take;
The clouds ye so much dread
Are big with mercy and shall break
In blessings on your head.

Judge not the Lord by feeble sense,
But trust Him for His grace;
Behind a frowning providence
He hides a smiling face.
His purposes will ripen fast,
Unfolding every hour;
The bud may have a bitter taste,
But sweet will be the flower.

Blind unbelief is sure to err
And scan His work in vain;
God is His own interpreter,
And He will make it plain."

CHAPTER 3

A Match Made in Heaven

Ephesians 1:3-4, 5:25-27

The World As a Stage

THE BOOK OF EPHESIANS puts us right in the middle of a drama. The world is the stage. It is the backdrop, the setting, the context where a grand, redemptive drama is unfolding. Seeing the world this way helps us get a glimpse of what God is out to accomplish through the mystery.

From before the world's formation to its consummation, Ephesians reveals that a marriage is at the center of the plot. It is not merely the remarriage of heaven and earth like we studied in the last chapter. This one is personal. Notice the parallel phrases in these verses found in Chapter 1 and Chapter 5 (emphasis mine):

> "For He chose us in Him, before the foundation of the world, ***to be holy and blameless*** in His sight" (1:4).

> "Husbands, love your wives, just as Christ loved the church and gave Himself for her to make her holy, cleansing her with

the washing of water by the word. He did this to present the church to Himself in splendor, without spot or wrinkle or anything like that, but **holy and blameless**" (5:25-27).

A holy and blameless people in Chapter 1 become the holy and blameless bride in Chapter 5. Connecting these dots reveals what was happening before the world began. A marriage had been ordained. A people were predestined to be a bride. The world set the stage. In love, God had chosen this holy and blameless bride for His Son.

A Wedding Sermon

Years ago when I was a college pastor, my summer weekends were filled with officiating wedding ceremonies. Below is a copy of one charge I gave to a couple, Pete and Katie, who were tying the knot. Looking back on those days, I remember how fun the ceremonies were. I loved seeing the joy on their faces. I loved holding up marriage as one great platform to tell people about the bigger marriage story going on in the world.

So just read along and imagine yourself witnessing this young couple, Pete and Katie, tie the knot. I hope this charge will help you see the marriage at the heart of human history.

> "Today is a great day because it is the culmination of a great story – one that I encourage you to cherish and remember often together. But today the Bible tells us in Ephesians 5 that this union we celebrate – this joining together of two into one – is just a faint whisper of a greater story. This beautiful ceremony, however perfect it is, is just an echo of a greater ceremony. And the many months of your romance offer a tiny glimpse of a greater romance that is told in the pages of Scripture.

The Apostle Paul lays out God's design for marriage and tells us of the most faithful, sacrificial love the world has ever known in Ephesians 5 – it's the love between Christ Jesus and His bride. Your union today, Paul tells us, is to be a reflection of the greatest union ever known - the union between Christ and His church.

This romance has been planned since before time began, in the depths of eternity, in the heart of a Being called the Trinity - God the Father, God the Son, and God the Spirit. God the Father declared a plan. In His love for His Son, He desired to bring a love-gift to Him. It was a tribute of sorts. This wouldn't be just any love gift. Not possessions, not riches though they will be involved, this gift would be a unique people – a spotless and blameless bride – to reflect His Son's worth and to be His Son's joy for all eternity.

In the letters of Titus and 2 Timothy, we read of God choosing a people before time began and revealing that this plan would be carried out in Christ Jesus, His Son. So before this world ever was, a great love story was unfolding. A people, set apart by God, would be given to His Son for His everlasting possession. God created the world and began with a marriage of two humans, Adam and Eve. But soon after this, Adam and Eve went their own way apart from God's wisdom and sinned. As a result, humanity fell from this blessed relationship with God. Estrangement and shame entered into the relationship which was created for glory and beauty. God, who once walked among His people, now had to distance Himself from them because His holiness could not tolerate their impurity.

God had planned something that the world would never expect. He planned that His very own Son would go to earth and give His life as a ransom for His bride. Her sin would cost Him His life. Just as in ancient times when parents would choose the mate and the husband-to-be would have to pay a dowry to redeem the bride for his own, we see God choosing the bride and the Son coming to pay the dowry. This wasn't just any dowry though. To buy this bride meant dying for her. So God's Son came to earth, clothed Himself with flesh, and died a totally undeserved death. Acts 20:28 tells us that Christ bought the church with His own blood. Ephesians 5:25 tells us that husbands should love their wives as Christ also loved the church and gave Himself up for her. So Jesus had to die to gain this bride. Death was the dowry.

Death wasn't the end though. God raised Him from the dead thereby declaring to the world that even death could not keep His Son. Death would not be a hindrance to this marriage. The romance wasn't over. The grave couldn't hold this Groom.

Jesus ascended into heaven a few days later and sent another helper, the Holy Spirit. Ephesians 1 tells us the Spirit acts as a sort of engagement ring. He is the promise of a better day coming. The Holy Spirit is to keep this love-gift until the day when the Son is reunited in perfect fullness with His bride. So the church waits for her wedding, just as you two have been anxiously waiting for so long for this day.

The Father set the plan, the Son accomplished it, and the Spirit secures it until the great day when the Groom and His bride reunite in perfect fullness.

We witness the wedding scene at the end of the Bible in Revelation 19:7-9 when a multitude in heaven shouts, "Let us rejoice and be glad and give the glory to Him, for the marriage of the Lamb has come and His bride has made herself ready...then he said to me, 'Write, "Blessed are those who are invited to the marriage supper of the Lamb."'" (NASU)

The Scriptures end with this vision – a bride and Groom reunited for all of eternity to enjoy each other and make much of Christ forever and ever.

Pete and Katie, I tell you this eternal romance because it is the reason we are gathered here today. This day would not exist if God had not planned to use marriage to be an earthly portrait of this heavenly reality. Your marriage exists solely to reflect and display a greater marriage. When it is all said and done, the test of your faithfulness in marriage will be how well you reflected this greater marriage to the world. Even the roles God has ordained for you in marriage point beyond themselves. Pete, you, as the loving, servant-minded leader tells the world of Christ's unending, sacrificial love. Katie, your role as the respectful, submissive wife tells the world of the joy it is to submit yourself and your future into the able hands of another just the church does to Christ. We charge you to be faithful today, not for your sake alone, but for the story you tell the world about the love of Christ for His bride. The mini-drama of your marriage reflects this greater marriage. Approach each day with a joyful, sober sacredness.

Congregation, the invitation to the greater wedding feast remains open to you. "Blessed are those who are invited to the marriage supper of the Lamb" John writes in Revelation (NASU). This invitation does not come on the basis of works. It is solely a gift. God cannot give you a seat to dine at this table if there is sin separating you from Him. What do I mean by sin? Sin is not loving God and not obeying His ways. Those who are invited to be the love gift from the Father to the Son are only those who clothe themselves in the fine linen of the righteousness of Christ by faith. They have to be made holy and blameless by His death on the cross. All you must do to have a seat at this feast and be invited to this wedding is to trust in Christ alone for the payment of your debt. He will dress you so that you can be holy and blameless before Him.

And congregation, the Bible tells us that no one knows when the Son will come again to redeem His bride. So please listen to the reason why we are here today. Pete and Katie are giving you a visual foreshadowing of what's coming when the church will be with Christ in one never-ending marriage where there is fullness of joy forever.

Those who know Christ and are gathered here today, I invite you just to relish the echo of this ceremony. Long for the day when you will hear this multitude that John heard. Long for the day when you will enter into unhindered union with Christ.

So, Pete and Katie, tell this incredible story with your marriage from this day forward and tell it well. The world is waiting to hear what you have to say."[5]

Marriage Displays the Mystery

Human marriage not only portrays this greater marriage, it also points beyond itself to the mystery in Ephesians. God lifts the veil on the mystery through marriage. Marriage gives us categories that enable us to see it, to sense it. That's why Paul can jump from human marriage to Christ and the church and even to the mystery so seamlessly.

Watch how marriage and the mystery flow from one to the other in these verses:

> "For this reason a man will leave his father and mother and be joined to his wife, and the two will become one flesh. This mystery is profound, but I am talking about Christ and the church" (Ephesians 5:31-32).

---

[5] Some of the texts and flow of this wedding sermon was helped by John Macarthur's sermon at the 2001 Shepherds Conference on Sanctification.

Genesis 2, which Paul quotes here, reveals God's blueprint for marriage: the two become one flesh. Sound familiar? Recall Chapter 1 of Ephesians. What is the end goal of the mystery? To bring two realms, heaven and earth, together as one in Jesus. The two become one in the mystery. The two also become one in marriage.

The point? God has used the canvas of marriage to paint a picture for us to see the mystery. The mystery's unifying dynamic is illustrated in marriage. God has lifted the veil, giving us a glimpse, of what lies at the heart of His mystery. Restoration of unity is central to both the mystery *and* the gospel in Ephesians. That is why Paul calls this news the "mystery of the gospel" in Ephesians 6:19. As Tim Keller states, marriage is a "gospel re-enactment."[6] Marriage retells the story. Marriage re-enacts God's unifying work through the gospel of Jesus Christ, which also forms the core of the mystery. Two joining as one mimics the reconciling dynamic of the mystery. Here's another way to say it: marriage illustrates the mystery by portraying the process while the gospel fuels the mystery by providing its power.

Reconciliation, at the core of the mystery, is made possible by the gospel and conceivable through the picture of marriage. Marriage is perfectly wired to display the mystery. Marriage befits the mystery. It is a match made in heaven, unveiled on earth.

---

[6] Tim and Kathy Keller, "Gospel Re-enacment: Cultivating a Healthy Marriage," teaching given on April 1, 2005 at Redeemer Presbyterian Church.

CHAPTER 4

The Veil Lifted by Christ's Victory

Ephesians 1:18-2:9, 4:7-10

The World As a Theater

WE HAVE SEEN THE world as a stage for redemption and romance from Ephesians 1. Ephesians 2 reveals the world as a theater — not a movie theater but a context for battle. The world is at war.

This war rages on but its noise, like the noise in a crowded coffee shop, goes on and on as the unrecognized backdrop of our lives. It surrounds us all the time, but we really don't hear it. We have never known a time when it did not exist, so our ears have grown accustomed to it.

Ephesians reveals that the noise of battle fills heaven and earth. The "buzz" is enmity and strife. This world is the theater where a cosmic war is unfolding. This is the war that is behind all other wars.

But two people knew what it was like without this noise. Adam and Eve knew peace until they made the tragic choice to join forces with God's enemy, the devil. After they sinned, God Himself ordained that a battle would run its course through human history. He promised the serpent, "I will put hostility between you and the woman, and between your seed and her seed" (Genesis 3:15a). This enmity has not ceased.

This is no petty conflict over secondary issues. The victor means life or death for the human race. The one crowned holds the future – our future – in his hands. If the seed of woman triumphs, the way home is re-opened. If Satan and his seed win, hope dies and death wins.

The danger of this war is that people feel safe. Every day and in every context of life, they walk into a battlefield unarmed and unprotected because they operate under the illusion of safety. In his book, *The Screwtape Letters,* C. S. Lewis exposed some of the hidden tactics of the devil. The book contains a series of lessons from an elder demon to a younger demon, showing him the ropes of how to keep his "patient" safely in his grip. One scene has the elder demon reprimanding the younger demon for being so thrilled about an actual war that had started. Real war has the dangerous potential of awakening humanity to be concerned about the other war, he argued. This vulnerability stemmed from the danger of real war taking away one of their best weapons: "contented worldliness." "Our policy, for the moment," Lewis writes on behalf of Screwtape, "is to conceal ourselves."[7] Fake war through movie theaters is fine. Entertainment deafens the soul. But real war amid the real theater in which we live? No way - too much potential to rock the boat according to this elder demon. It unsettles the settled soul. War turns up the volume on the noise of battle, threatening to uncover the core battle behind it all.

With that battle in mind, let us read the beginning of Ephesians 2:

> "And you were dead in your trespasses and sins in which
> you previously walked according to the ways of this world,

---

[7] C. S. Lewis, *The Screwtape Letters,* Quality Print Book Club, United States of America, 1941, pgs. 32-39.

according to the ruler who exercises authority over the lower heavens, the spirit now working in the disobedient. We too all previously lived among them in our fleshly desires, carrying out the inclinations of our flesh and thoughts, and we were by nature children under wrath as the others were also" (2:1-3).

Before we focus on who wins this battle, let's locate our place in the struggle. We were not mere spectators. Paul reminds the Christians at Ephesus that they formerly enlisted themselves in the war. Did you catch this in Chapter 2? Lost humanity marches to Satan's orders, living "according to the ruler who exercises authority over the lower heavens" (2:2b). Before we believed, we had joined forces. This obedience is not forced upon us from the outside. We willingly submitted: "We too all previously lived among them in our fleshly desires, carrying out the inclinations of our flesh and thoughts, and we were by nature children under wrath as the others were also" (2:3). We wholeheartedly ran from God. Our flesh aligned nicely with Satan's forces. We loved the darkness over the light.

Paul labels these evil angelic forces who oppose Christ in Chapter 6 as "authorities," "rulers," and even "world powers of this darkness" (Ephesians 6:12). These forces have joined themselves with the "ruler who exercises authority in the lower heavens" who is the spirit that instigates disobedience against God (Ephesians 2:1-3). They operate in the darkness, sometimes visibly and sometimes invisibly. Humanity and angelic hosts declared mutiny against God, and it's a collaborative effort. Heaven and earth have formed an alliance against God and His Christ.

Notice that Paul describes the devil as "the ruler" who exercises authority over the lower heavens. This is the realm in which we live and move. The world as we know it is under the authority of the evil one. He wields his limited authority to create an environment where defiance to God is celebrated and righteousness denigrated. Adam relegated this position to him. The devil energizes disobedience to God by tempting people with the empty promise of "more." Through worldliness, he numbs people to the reality of their condition and the reality of the war. It is the noise that goes unnoticed in a world gone wrong. More knowledge, more happiness, more power, more everything. His tactics remain the same: "You will be like God, knowing . . ." (Genesis 3:5b). God is ultimately sovereign and superintends the conflict, but for now, He has given the evil one a certain amount of limited authority over this world. This is his domain. The Bible, however uneasy this may feel, labels him the "god of this age" in 2 Corinthians 4:4. The theater for this conflict is enemy turf. The devil and his heavenly opposition will not give up their ground easily.

Ephesians 2:1-3 reminds the Christians that this "life" they lived was actually death. Our supposed freedom was actually slavery. "And you were dead in your trespasses and sins . . ." (2:1). We crossed the line. We severed the tie. In our former defiance, we cut ourselves off from the Life-giver. We chose the creation over the Creator. This defiance was death.

This cosmic alliance stands against God's reunification effort of bringing everything together in the Messiah. Two, heaven and earth, have come against the One. This army opposes the mystery. Death, defiant humanity, the devil, demons, darkness, this domain itself – all of them unite against God's plan of unity. The odds seem stacked in their favor. The theater for war, it seems, will soon be at "peace" under the dominion of darkness.

Or will it? It is into this fray, straight into the frontlines that God sent His Warrior Son, the seed of Eve.

Christ the Overcomer

The outcome of the war was clear from the day humanity joined the ranks - all the way back in Genesis 3. Satan is haunted by the words he heard that day: "He will strike your head, and you will strike his heel." He did not know when, where, how, or even who, but he knew his day was coming and his doom was sure. The nearness of that dreadful day began settling in while Jesus lived on earth. They had never faced someone like Him. This is why the demons in the gospel of Mark start making their bucket list in front of Jesus in Chapter 5:6-12. Entering pigs only makes the cut if absolute terror has taken over. They beg Jesus for more time precisely because they know they operate on borrowed time. This certain defeat was like a gloomy cloud that followed these evil forces everywhere. Even the darkness wasn't light to them.

And now those fears have become reality. God's promised Warrior has come. This evil alliance has met its match. The Victor has been crowned. Paul takes us to the deciding moment in Ephesians 1:20-23:

> "He [God] demonstrated this power in the Messiah by rais-
> ing Him from the dead and seating Him at His right hand
> in the heavens - far above every ruler and authority, power
> and dominion, and every title given, not only in this age
> but also in the one to come. And He put everything under
> His feet and appointed Him as head over everything for the
> church, which is His body, the fullness of the One who fills
> all things in every way."

God's power raised Jesus from the dead. Death's power lay defeated. God's power seated Christ in the heavens. Christ proved too much for Satan. God's power subjected everything under Jesus' feet, reasserting the order that was Eden. The deed to this world has been transferred into the Name of Another. It's over. Christ entered the theater. He won on their turf, and His triumph has been declared for all to see. Christ has conquered and been crowned.

With His enemies at His feet, His greatness exceeds all. Christ reigns in unparalleled glory with ultimate authority.

When God turned the tides and raised Christ from the dead, it signaled something new was here. It lifted the veil of the mystery. Before that, every warrior had yielded to death's power. Abraham, Joseph, Moses, David - the heroes of old were no match. But the bodily resurrection of Jesus altered the story. The empty tomb rendered the devil's three-day boast empty. The world began a different trajectory that day. The devil's own weapon had turned against him in defeat. The author of Hebrews tells us, "Through [Jesus'] death He might destroy the one holding the power of death - that is the devil" (2:14b). The resurrection vindicated Jesus' claim to the throne and declared Him to be God's Son in power (Romans 1:4).

God then took Jesus on a victory march through the heavens. Paul records that God seated Him "at His right hand in the heavens -far above every ruler and authority, power and dominion, and every title given, not only in this age but also in the one to come. And He put everything under His feet and appointed Him as head over everything for the church" (1:20b-22).

This momentous turn of events was the watershed moment that unleashed the mystery into the world. Christ re-established the ordered world of Eden when He triumphed over His foes. He is the new Adam. Paul quotes from Psalm 8 when he states that God "put everything under His feet." The hope captured in that psalm moved from prophecy to reality that day. A path for earth to be invaded by heaven was paved that day. A new world of possibilities was born.

I recently talked to a friend whose "life" had been crushed by a sin that he had hidden for years. He tearfully wanted everything back the way it was. Sin had wrecked the life he once knew. Sleep evaded him. Fears haunted him. Guilt chased him. One night, as he was sleeping, he dreamed that life had returned to normal. He awoke and realized that in reality, a nightmare awaited him every day.

That is like reading Psalm 8. The world envisioned there is like the dream. We do not wake up to a world where all is at rest. We live the nightmare that we have created by our sin. We live in a world in disarray. When our eyes pass over the peaceful orderliness of "shalom" like Psalm 8 articulates, we wish we would never wake up. We wish we were living the dream. The world turned right side up sounds so appealing in this world turned upside down.

> "What is man that You remember him, the son of man that You look after him? You made him little less than God and crowned him with glory and honor. You made him lord over the works of Your hands; You put everything under his feet: all the sheep and oxen, as well as the animals in the wild, the birds of the sky, and the fish of the sea that pass through the currents of the seas" (Psalm 8:4-8).

Psalm 8 thrills the imagination with what will be. All the world once again submits to mankind as it was designed to. Man submits to God. The harmony of Eden restored. But it exists in the realm of the "not yet." The author of Hebrews captures the distance of that world and our current vantage point with this stinging reminder: "As it is, we do not yet see everything subjected to him" (2:8b). The vision of Psalm 8 lies in the future. We ache for that day but we still dwell here, in this fallen world.

But not Jesus. He has entered into this place of glory and honor. He has pioneered the path and reached the destination. Suffering has led to glory. That is the ascension. His world is in order. He now reigns with all things under His feet. He no longer lives the nightmare. His position guarantees the world will be reordered. The old Adam's dark shadow has yielded to the light of the New. The "dream" of Psalm 8 has begun working itself out in reality. The lines between present suffering and future glory have been blurred by the ascension of Jesus. The future has come. We see a new world in Jesus' sovereignty - a world where the mystery has become reality. A world where the veil has been removed.

This is why Christ's ascension remains so central in Ephesians. If this letter were a story, the pivotal, plot-changing moments would be the end of Chapter 1 and Chapter 4. Those texts focus on that event - that triumphant moment when Christ's enemies fell crippled to His feet and He ascended on high. In Chapter 1, God announces His reclamation of what was rightfully His by declaring His Son King, giving Him the Name above all names. In Chapter 4, we read, "When He ascended on high, He took prisoners into captivity; He gave gifts to people . . . The One who descended is also the One who ascended far above all the heavens, that He might fill all things" (4:8, 10). Christ's ascension unleashed God's plan of restoration.

Notice this text in 4:10 again: "That He might fill all things." The goal of the Son of God's dwelling among humanity as a human, the goal of His descent was to fill "all things." His filling all things is the result of His finishing His mission on earth.[8] This is the accomplishment of the ascension. There is nothing left to be done; all is at rest.

Well, almost. This filling is not yet complete. The world has yet to taste of His fullness. The mystery has yet to reach its climax when everything comes together in Psalm 8 fashion. Jesus has entered into His rest, but the church has not. She still dwells in the midst of the darkness that remains. He has yet to bring her to the fullness of His conquest. So Christ, as head over all, turns His energies to the church, His body that remains on earth. God "appointed Him as head over everything for the church" (Ephesians 1:22). He doesn't leave her to navigate the path to glory on her own. His power energizes the church. He exercises His sovereignty "for" her. This means the church is the present context where Christ's kingly power can be witnessed on earth. He showers her with heavenly blessings so she finds all she needs to endure. The church is a glimpse, however faint it may be, of heaven on earth.

---

[8] From personal correspondence with Andy.

Chapter 2 of Ephesians reveals how Jesus uses His authority for the church's good. He announces His victory through rescuing sinners and reconciling enemies. God initiates the mystery by graciously reuniting with man through Jesus (Ephesians 2:1-10) and reconciling man to man in Jesus (Ephesians 2:11-22). The mystery has begun in Jesus' restoration of unity in our vertical relationship to God and our horizontal relationships with one another. This would be impossible without Christ's triumphant ascent to the Father's right hand.

Christ's victory has its trophies in both heaven and earth. The heavenly realm witnesses Christ's accomplishments in those who are sharers in His victory. Watch how this unfolds in Ephesians 2:1-9:

> "And you were dead in your trespasses and sins in which you previously walked according to the ways of this world, according to the ruler who exercises authority over the lower heavens, the spirit now working in the disobedient. We too all previously lived among them in our fleshly desires, carrying out the inclinations of our flesh and thoughts, and we were by nature children under wrath as the others were also. But God, who is rich in mercy, because of His great love that He had for us, made us alive with the Messiah even though we were dead in trespasses. You are saved by grace! Together with Christ Jesus He also raised us up and seated us in the heavens, so that in the coming ages He might display the immeasurable riches of His grace through His kindness to us in Christ Jesus. For you are saved by grace through faith, and this is not from yourselves; it is God's gift— not from works, so that no one can boast."

By an act of God's mercy, a sinful people follow Christ's footsteps now. The path He tread has now opened before them. Tasting Christ's glory, they are dead, raised, and then seated in the heavens with Him (2:6-7).

Heaven witnesses Christ's victory. Grace rescued these sinners from the losing team. The earth witnesses Christ's victory through the new community Christ has created, the church (Ephesians 2:11-22). The cosmos has become the trophy room of the Messiah. The mystery has begun.

CHAPTER 5

The Heavenly Unveiling

Ephesians 1:18-2:10

SEPTEMBER 11, 2001 SHOOK the world as we knew it. When the dust settled, a lingering unsettledness remained. The foundational categories to any society - mutual trust and innate self-preservation - were challenged by radical extremists. A new war was at hand. In the wake of those events, America instituted a scale of measuring the terror threat level by which its citizens are made aware of imminent attacks to national security. There are five categories of relative risk. The worldwide monitoring of terrorist networks helps them gauge if an attack seems likely. If chatter increases and a specific attack emerges, authorities alert American citizens by simply raising the level. It sends a signal to all Americans to be on the alert.

Likewise, but with the attackers on the defense and peace being the goal, a similar signal keeps going out to the heavens in Ephesians. In Ephesians Chapter 2, the evil, angelic forces feel the imminent threat. Their threat level never downgrades but remains in the critical zone, at level five. Christ's victory keeps penetrating enemy lines. God keeps redeeming sinners through Him. The Victor is on the move. Unsettled and fearful, these heavenly hosts keep hearing the chatter of Christ's first tactical move to unleash the mystery.

Death Overcome by Life

Chapter 2 of Ephesians reveals the spoils of Christ's triumph. Christ's victory is such a momentous event that it can't be contained. God keeps sending shockwaves through the heavens, re-announcing Christ's victory over and over again through reclaiming people for Himself. The trophies that laud His accomplishments keep piling up.

All believers have become Christ's heavenly trophies. Christ has reconciled them to God. They are the reason the evil heavenly hosts keep looking over their shoulders. Look at our heavenly status in Ephesians 2:4-6:

> "But God, who is rich in mercy, because of His great love that He had for us, made us alive with the Messiah even though we were dead in trespasses. You are saved by grace! Together with Christ Jesus He also raised us up and seated us in the heavens."

We still live on earth, but we also share Christ's victory and heavenly authority by God's mercy and grace. There is more to our lives than merely what we see with our eyes.

Our presence in the heavenlies points to Christ's achievements because our stories echo His. Precisely the way God saved Him is how God saves us. God repeats what He did with Jesus: "raising" us from the dead and "seating" us in the heavenlies. These same terms that describe Christ in 1:20-23 describe the believers in 2:4-6. Our presence in the heavenlies showcases Christ's glory and God's mercy. Reconciled, redeemed believers are the heavenly unveiling of God's initial phase of the mystery.

The places where Christ's story converges with ours are intentional on God's part. He has scripted the whole story to revolve around Jesus. But one important distinction must be made. Our victory flows from grace. Christ's victory is the recognition of merit. He deserved the prize He received. He earned the title "Victor" because He battled and won. His record spoke for itself. God honored Him by raising Him and crowning Him king. Christ took the seat that was rightfully His.

Believers share in Christ's victory in Chapter 2 of Ephesians even though they had no right to be on the winning side. Nothing inherent in us merited victory. Actually it's just the opposite. Judgment was rightfully ours: "And you were dead in your trespasses and sins in which you previously walked according to the ways of this world" (2:1-2a). Christ died in obedience. Our death resulted from disobedience and issued forth more disobedience. As sinners, Paul reminds us that we had chosen sides against God. We who are in Christ deserved to lose, forever. "But God, who is rich in mercy . . ." (Ephesians 2:4).

Grace appeared. Out of the abundance of His merciful heart, God opened the storehouse of Christ's spoils to sinners like us. He imparts Christ's resurrected life and Christ's regal authority to undeserving believers. By God's free grace, we are declared participants of Christ's victory, redeemed from Satan's authority, and released from indulging the flesh. Paul's lengthy list of God's richest treasures in Chapter 1 became ours when faith united us to Christ.

This is what "saved" means in Ephesians 2:9a: "For you are saved by grace through faith." Saved from the wrath we deserve, saved from the dominion of darkness we served, saved from the death we chose. He saved us "so that in the coming ages He might display the immeasurable riches of His grace through His kindness to us in Christ Jesus" (2:7). Rich is God's mercy. Great is His love. Victory is ours. Christ is ours.

This past tense in Ephesians 2:1-3 reminds us that if God had not mercifully interrupted our worldly indulgence, we would still be hopelessly lost. Believers *were* children of wrath, Paul writes, but now they enjoy the wealth of God's glorious grace. Believers *were* under the dominion of the devil but now they share in Christ's dominion.

Once alienated by sin and guilt, now we are reunited with God through Christ. The two, separated by sin and guilt, have become one through Christ. Death has proven no match for Christ's indestructible life. The heavenly hosts witness this first unveiling of God's mystery and shudder. The chatter never stops. They cannot hold Him back. This vertical unity between God and man reveals that the mystery has begun repairing what sin divided and nothing can stop it.

Christ's victory parade is not over. God's mystery presses on.

Boasting Overwhelmed by Grace

These believers make an odd trophy case to display Christ's triumph. Trophies usually center attention directly on the recipient's accomplishments. A trophy's bent is toward proving the legitimacy of the recipient's boast - what they won, whom they beat, and how they beat them. Not these. Not the believers in Ephesians 2. They don't taunt their opponents. They don't laud their own accomplishments. Grace distinguishes them from all others. They deflect attention to Another. We received the victory, but we did not earn it. Christ's accomplishments on our behalf form our boast, our crown, and our joy. It's a strange way to win in this world where self-exaltation is the goal of victory. But grace mixes glory with humility. Our heavenly exaltedness in Christ produces an earthly lowliness.

In Ephesians 1 we overheard one of these "trophies" singing his song of victory. The thrice-repeated refrain, "praise to His glory," formed the content of his boast (1:6, 12, 14). Paul's victory song deflected attention to God's greatness and Christ's supremacy, not his own.

This boasting in Christ alone is music to the Father's ears. He designed the gospel to function this way: "For you are saved by grace through faith, and this is not from yourselves; it is God's gift – not from works, so that no one can boast" (2:8-9).

The gospel silences our innate self-exalting, self-enamored ways of thinking and behaving. It kills pride that blends "self-absorption - that is narcissism – with an overestimate of one's abilities or worth – that is conceit. So a proud person thinks a lot *about* herself and also thinks a lot *of* herself."[9] The gospel works upon people in exactly the opposite way: they start thinking a lot about Another and have a sober view of themselves.

Notice the boast-emptying goal of grace in Ephesians 2:9-10: "For you are saved by grace through faith, and this is not from yourselves, it is God's gift – not from works, so that no one can boast." In salvation, Christ's righteousness is credited to us in such a way that no credit can be taken by us. It's all on Him. Salvation comes from outside us, not from within us. The shocking freeness of God's gift renders us undone. Salvation comes by grace through faith, and even the faith itself is granted by God. When free grace fills the heart, self-preoccupation yields to praise. Boasting has been overwhelmed by grace.

My family of six loves some coupons. A few years ago, we were given some coupons to McDonald's for two free Big Macs. My wife and I were enjoying the Big Macs while my son enjoyed his regular hamburger. I looked

---

[9] Plantinga, Cornelius, *Not the Way It's Supposed to Be: A Breviary of Sin*, Wm. B. Eerdmans Publishing Co., 1995. pg. 80.

at Owen and held my Big Mac beside his cheeseburger and said, "Owen, look how much bigger my burger is." Without a second of hesitation, my daughter Emma, who was four at the time, quickly stepped in to remind me, "Umm. Daddy, we shouldn't boast." Ouch. Needless to say that wasn't one of my finer moments in fatherhood. Think about how silly it was of me to boast. First of all, a 30-year-old feels the need to one-up a three-year-old? Hmm. Second of all, it's a hamburger. Meat, sauce, and bread. That's all. I didn't make the burger. I didn't have one hand in the grains that made the bread, the tomatoes and whatever else that makes that special sauce, or much less the raising of the cows that became the beef. I was boasting about something I had no share in creating. Thirdly, I was boasting about something I "bought" with a coupon! A coupon that someone gave to me! Boasting had no place.

The freeness of that gift made my boast so foolish. But we do the same, don't we? We take the gifts we have received and turn them into reasons for self-promotion and self-confidence. Or we consider what we haven't received and grumble because someone else received what we think we really deserved. Self-pity and self-promotion are merely two sides of the same coin. Either way, we forget the freeness of it all. In Jesus we are flooded with grace that we could not earn and did not deserve. If boasting had no place in McDonald's that day, how much more is this true in our churches? Paul's words to Corinth apply to us, "What do you have that you didn't receive? If, in fact, you did receive it, why do you boast as if you hadn't received it?" (1 Corinthians 4:7b). Boasting has lost its glamour in the light of free grace. Boasting yields to praise in the community that understands the freeness of grace. Emma was right. We shouldn't boast.

Because the outward look to Christ captivates the heart, grace silences insecurity. This salvation is not centered on what we have, don't have, do, or don't do. It cures our need for comparative righteousness or blessedness. We are equally deserving of judgment, equally undeserving of salvation. We were "by nature children under wrath as the others were also" (Ephesians

2:3b). But God, being rich in mercy, because of His great love has done the unthinkable. We did everything to be excluded, and He mercifully included us in Christ. This strips the need for comparison. Comparing our lot to others' orients the posture of our soul toward what we don't have, instead of all that we do. It forgets grace. An older gentleman I used to see serving the church understood this truth. Every time I asked him, "How are you?" he would quickly reply, "Better than I deserve." Amen, brother. Amen. That is everyone's lot in Jesus.

"Why should I gain from His reward?" is the question posed by Stuart Townend in the hymn entitled, "How Deep the Father's Love for Us." Here is the wrong answer: look at your impressive resume or at another's unimpressive resume to find the answer. Stuart nailed the right answer with the next line: "I cannot give an answer." That sounds a lot like Paul when he wrote that salvation is "not from yourselves, it is God's gift" (Ephesians 2:9b). Answerless hearts have found the answer in Jesus. Praise fills the void in answerless heart. Grace overwhelms the boastful heart.

This is what the gospel does. It magnifies Christ by producing this paradox of crushed boldness.[10] Grace floods the heart in such a way that there is simply no room left for boasting.

This heavenly unveiling of God's mystery – the saints who are seated with Christ – puts the rest of the cosmos on alert. Death could not hold them. Pride no longer appeals to them. These trophies send the signal that creation's restoration has begun. Reconciled to God, they sing His song of victory.

---

[10] Doug Wilson, Blog and Mablog, Hebrews 3 Meditation, Date Unknown.

CHAPTER 6

The Earthly Unveiling

Ephesians 2:11-22

I T WAS TIME FOR the big reveal. During the summer of 2010, the sports world seemed to stand still. Every sports news show centered on the details concerning LeBron James' big decision. Where would King James land? The suspense finally ended when he announced he would be "taking his talents to South Beach" and joining the Miami Heat. The front office had pulled off a miracle. A dynasty was in view. The "Big 3" of LeBron, Dwayne Wade, and Chris Bosh promised total dominance. Just the announcement itself sent teams scrambling to beef up their talent in view of the newly stacked team in South Beach.

But the big decision was followed by a flood of criticism. The way LeBron and the Heat made the announcement disillusioned many. The announcement itself came across as though they thought they had the championship rings in hand but the season had yet to begin. The presumption and hubris turned LeBron from superstar to villain in a matter of hours.

Another "big reveal" happens in Ephesians 2:11-22. Only this time, the announcement is no pompous display of merely the hope of victory. It is the signal that the victory has been won. This earthly unveiling really does mean that the championship ring is already in hand. The ripple effect of this earthly trophy has the potential to send the world into a state of disillusionment, not with Christ, but with everything that stands against Him. It is a unity so real, yet so rare, that it sends people scrambling for answers. The big reveal happens to be the church.

Really? The big announcement is the church? Talk about drawing some criticism! Not for its hubris but for its weakness! The church seems to be an unimpressive way to announce that a dynasty had begun.

But is she? Maybe there is more to the church than the human eye can see.

Reconciled believers were the heavenly trophies of Christ in Ephesians 2:1-10. Ephesians 2:11-22 reveals that the church comprises the earthly trophy of the Messiah. This new community is where Christ's accomplishments are on display for the world to see.

One particular aspect of the church that lauds Christ's victory lies in the peace He created between former enemies. Peace has already transformed the relationship between God and man in Chapter 2. They who were "children of wrath" have been reconciled to God through Christ (2:3b-6). This vertical peace then finds its earthly counterpart in Chapter 2:11-22. Another hostility has ended. This time it is between man and man.

This earthly reconciliation, or in the language of Ephesians - this "two becoming one" – brings us back to Chapter 1 where the mystery's apex involved the two realms, heaven and earth, also becoming one in Christ. The church's unity in Chapter 2 then becomes a foretaste of the day when divisions will finally cease. Her oneness foreshadows the future oneness promised in the mystery. She is the preview of the film that's yet to be released. This future has invaded the present through Christ's conquest. Earth knocks on heaven's door in the church. This is why Charles Spurgeon called the church the "dearest place"[11] on earth. Even in all her imperfections, she remains a foretaste of glory.

We probably struggle to regard the church as dearly as Spurgeon did. But, let's take a step back and behold the wonder who is the church. Her existence evidences the mystery. Her very being signals the end is near. The church isn't a detour in God's program for the universe. She is His vehicle that advances His agenda for the world.

If you struggle to see her value, one way to begin esteeming her is to realize just what had to happen in order for her to exist. Let's read Ephesians 2:11-22 to start unpacking some of obstacles that Christ overcame in His creation of the church.

> "So then, remember that at one time you were Gentiles in the flesh—called "the uncircumcised" by those called "the circumcised," which is done in the flesh by human hands. At that time you were without the Messiah, excluded from the citizenship of Israel, and foreigners to the covenants of the promise, without hope and without God in the world. But now in Christ Jesus, you who were far away have been brought near by the blood of the Messiah. For He is our peace, who made both groups one and tore down the dividing wall of hostility. In His flesh, He made of no effect the law consisting of commands and expressed in regulations, so that He might create in Himself one new man from the two, resulting in peace. He did this so that He might reconcile both to God in one body through the cross and put the hostility to death by it. When the Messiah came, He proclaimed the good news of peace to you who were far away and peace to those who were near. For through Him we

---

[11] Charles Spurgeon, "Best Donation," a sermon delivered on April 5, 1891 at the Metropolitan Tabernacle in London, England.

both have access by one Spirit to the Father. So then you are no longer foreigners and strangers, but fellow citizens with the saints, and members of God's household, built on the foundation of the apostles and prophets, with Christ Jesus Himself as the cornerstone. The whole building, being put together by Him, grows into a holy sanctuary in the Lord. You also are being built together for God's dwelling in the Spirit."

Enmity Overcome by Peace

Sin separates. It carries within it an inherently boastful, prideful bent that separates man from God and man from man. Alienation and strife result. On the heels of the first sin, Cain's murder of Abel illustrated this blood-thirsty enmity. Sin birthed a rivalry that would rather dig a grave than be a brother's keeper. This selfish wedge between man and man rears its ugly head in all generations, among all cultures. Racism and segregation still divide us. The cultural elite suppress. The culturally downtrodden react. Husbands abuse their wives. One is judged by the color of his skin. Another by his birth family. The list goes on and on. Just watch the news and tell me this: where can man find peace on earth?

More education won't fix it. More civilized ways of thinking will merely create craftier sinners. It's sin that robs the world of peace. We are rebels toward God and rivals toward each other. Sin shrivels the soul so that its own needs, wants, and desires are placed above everyone else's. This innate enmity destroys any chance of unity.

As self-absorbed sinners, we view other people in one of two ways: either as threats to our desires or avenues to fulfill them. "Me" shapes the "we." We either flee from people who are perceived threats or we use people to fulfill our perceived needs. They either become the idol we hope in or the obstacle to the idol we want. If they are the obstacle to what we want, then we either run over them (Cain with Abel) or run from them (Esau with Jacob). Alienation results. If we cling to them not as the threat but as the promised providers of the pleasures we crave, our "unity" reaches only as deep as our selfish desire. As soon as they can't provide the answer to our "need" (which is pretty close to always), we stiff-arm them and go hunting for our next victim of choice. Once again, division occurs. Truly satisfying relationships elude us because the "me" governs the "we."

One age-old illustration of this rivalry becomes apparent in the Bible between the Jews and Gentiles. The Bible is full of examples of the hostility of this relationship. The Jews felt secure because they saw themselves as on the "inside" of God's grace and favor while the Gentiles were the outsiders, outcasts even. This Jewish pride in its own Jewishness drove a rift between these two groups that isolated them from each other for centuries. The Gentiles also joined in. They pushed back on Jewish presumption by warring against them, exiling them, and suppressing them over and over.

The Jewish feeling of security proved to be mere presumption. In their "chosen" status, they turned this favor upside down into a reason for ethnic pride and boasting. Instead of seeing God as special for choosing them, they looked at themselves as special and started feeling worthy of His choice. God had given Israel many privileges – the Law, His covenants, His promises, even the Messiah Himself came from their privileged race. But the sinful heart turned these gracious privileges into bonus points on a resume for self-promotion.

Even the gift of the Law, given to them as a good gift by God Himself, was used by sin to reinforce this self-righteousness. God's laws were intended to separate Israel from the rest of the nations, but this cultural space was not intended to produce cultural superiority. The Law was in fact meant to distinguish them as special, not because of race but because of grace. Their special status was meant to showcase God's special grace so that the nations would turn their eyes toward God. Instead, Israel used it as a platform to start looking down on the nations. Sin used this wall as a means of cultural seclusion and cultural suppression. Thus, Paul labels the Law the "dividing wall of hostility" in Ephesians 2:14.

The "have-nots" in the Jewish mindset, deserved what they had coming to them. The Gentiles, those not physically related to the line of Abraham, were excluded. "Amen" they might say. The Gentiles lacked the inroads to the promises of God and the people of God. Sin flipped the farness of the Gentiles on its head by engendering a sense of prideful presumption in Israel's own status as "near" (Ephesians 2:13, 17).

The story of Jonah illustrates the deep-rootedness of this hostility. Jonah was perfectly content for God's mercy to save him via the fish. But when God extended mercy to the Gentiles, he became indignant. They had no right to mercy! His bitterness over the broadness of God's mercy takes him lower and lower until he finally prays, "And now, LORD, please take my life from me, for it is better for me to die than to live" (Jonah 4:3b). Jonah would rather die than share. And I thought my kids were bad. Here is God's prophet!

Jonah's anger with the wideness of God's mercy to the Ninevites reveals the conflict at the core of the human dilemma. We turn God's mercies into mirrors for our self-worth. "He saved me because I am good at this or that," we inwardly boast. God's mercy then becomes a platform to promote our superiority and justify our suppression of others. Jonah's refusal to open his arms as wide as God's to embrace undeserving Gentiles reveals how he inwardly believed he earned the claim to God's mercy. He had a "right" they didn't (and couldn't and shouldn't) have. It was fair of God to save him, but how could He save them?

Jonah missed the point of the fish. God's grace doesn't review résumés to see who is worthy. Everyone is unworthy. If God were fair, we would all be finished. This is Paul's point when reminded the Jewish Christians at Ephesus, "And we were by nature children under wrath as the others were also" (Ephesians 2:3b). The "others" in this verse refers to the Gentiles. Paul agrees; they were under wrath. But Paul reminds the Christians with Jewish roots that they too were under wrath. Both groups are equally undeserving.

I was watching a basketball game one night that was nearing the end. One announcer, I believe it was Clark Kellogg for CBS, used a phrase I will never forget. One of the best players on the court was called for his fifth foul and this was Clark's description of this player being disqualified: "He's been dairy-queened." Disqualified. DQ'd. The game was over for him; it was time for him to take his seat on the bench. If Jonah looked in the mirror with any degree of honesty, he would have realized both he and the Ninevites had been "dairy-queened." DQ'd. They were both running from God when God stepped in to rescue them.

Jonah's anger shows the depth of this wedge between these age-old rivals. It is right into this deeply engrained ethnic hostility that Christ entered to preach peace in Ephesians 2. God didn't send Him into the outskirts of the battle but right into the center. If Christ could overcome the wall of division between Jews and Gentiles that would mean His redemption would have altered something deep within both groups. If that towering wall could crumble, all others can too. Christ, unlike Jonah, didn't come reluctantly. He crossed over from his "culture" to those who had been designated outsiders: "When the Messiah came, He proclaimed the good news of peace to you who were far away and peace to those who were near" (Ephesians 2:17). The "outsiders" *and* the "insiders" needed peace preached to them. They both needed rescuing.

This self-righteous bent needed overcoming if the mystery was to be released on earth. Self-righteousness may not feel like enmity toward others, but it produces false categories that reinforce the walls that separate man from man. If the mystery, God's program to bring unity, is to be unveiled to the earth, then this wall must come down. This enmity must be overcome with peace.

And that's exactly what Jesus did. He came and ushered peace into this hostility. He created a third race based on grace and not race.

Ephesians 2:11-22 reveals this truth with the words themselves but Paul also employs a structure that reinforces this truth. Christ's peace-creating, wall-crumbling victory is displayed in two ways. The sentences *tell* us what Christ did. The structure *shows* us what He did. The purposeful ordering of the words themselves paint a picture of a wall and Christ's triumphant march around this "Jericho" to bring it down. The marks of isolation Paul rehearses in 2:11-12 are replaced with signs of inclusion in 2:18-20. The force of Christ's triumph over this hostility begins settling in as a complete reversal has happened. The community excluded from the "citizenship of Israel" in 2:12 has been made "fellow citizens with the saints" in 2:19 in Christ. "Foreigners to the covenants of promise" in 2:12 have been brought in to be "no longer foreigners" in 2:19.

These reversals form the outer edge of the structural pattern I mentioned earlier. If you venture in from these edges to the center of verses 11-22, in verse 14b, you hit a wall. Both in the words themselves and the structure the words create, there sits the barrier that keeps the two groups as "two." That's where Christ's glory is seen. He tears down the "wall of hostility" and changes the makeup of who comprises God's community. The two have become one in Him because the wall is no more. Peace has overcome hostility. Christ abolished the wall that stood between us. Right after the wall in the middle of this structure is torn down, Paul articulates Christ's purpose was so that "He might create in Himself one new man from the two, resulting in peace" (Ephesians 2:15).

This Jericho moment means the earth is beginning to be enveloped by God's mystery. The wall has come down. God has lifted the veil. The fallout of this momentous event was that a new people have been created. The church's unity displays the mystery. This indeed is a "big reveal."

Division Overcome by Unity

In Ephesians 2:14-15, Paul shows the wall that stood in the way of God's plan of unity. Its presence reinforced the divisiveness that mandated the two remain two. Oneness was impossible without removing the wall.

This wall represented everything anti-mystery in the world. Everything fallen and sinful and divisive about the human race was sadly illustrated there. As a structure itself, as it was the "law consisting of commands" it wasn't bad but "holy, righteous, and good" (Ephesians 2:15a; Romans 7:7-12). But sin perverted its purpose. Sin exploited it, using the wall of commandments to produce death and division.

Paul writes concerning that wall, "In His [Christ's] flesh, He made of no effect the law consisting of commands and expressed in regulations, so that He might create in Himself one new man from the two, resulting in peace" (Ephesians 2:15). The two are now one. The old is now new. Paul hit this same note with the believers at Colossae when he wrote, "And when you were dead in trespasses and in the uncircumcision of your flesh, He made you alive with Him and forgave us all our trespasses. He erased the certificate of debt, with its obligations, that was against us and opposed to us, and has taken it out of the way by nailing it to the cross" (Colossians 2:13-14). The way has been opened because the wall has been taken out of the way. What stood contrary to us has now been conquered by Christ. Unity has overcome disunity through Christ. A new community has been created.

Notice the togetherness that marks the end of Chapter 2 and the beginning of Chapter 3 of Ephesians (emphasis mine):

> "For through Him we **both** have access by **one** Spirit to the Father" (2:18).

"So then you are no longer foreigners and strangers, but *fellow* citizens **with** the saints, and members of God's household, built on the foundation of the apostles and prophets, with Christ Jesus Himself as the cornerstone" (2:19-20).

"You also are being built **together** for God's dwelling in the Spirit" (2:22).

"The Gentiles are **coheirs**, members of the **same** body, and **partners** of the promise in Christ Jesus through the gospel" (3:6).

Sound familiar? It's the dynamic of the mystery: two becoming one. The church evidences it. Marriage portrays it. History itself is being driven toward it. Forged together as one: that's God's banner for the mystery.

The destruction of the wall opened the possibility for this togetherness. This new people are reunited to God and to each other through Christ. Unity has invaded a world at war.

Remember how marriage naturally displays the mystery's dynamic of unity? The "two becoming one" mirrors the unifying dynamic of the mystery. It's a no-brainer. It's a match made in heaven, literally. But that's not the case with this portrait of the mystery in Ephesians. The making of these former enemies into one new community doesn't happen naturally. This unveiling surprises everyone. All cultures have categories for marriage. But this new community? No way. This unity stands out. The world didn't see this one coming.

Writing this book took me to some great coffee shops. During the rush one day, people were coming in and out, in and out. The bell on the door kept ringing. The music was blaring. Espresso machines roared in the background. Everyone's volume slowly and subtly had to rise to compensate. Every noise increased the volume but nothing stood out. It all mushed together in this buzz. Then it happened. A two-year-old boy belly-laughed. He was being tickled by his mother and just couldn't hold it in. This was a full-out, tear-dropping, "I can't stop" kind of laugh. It was pure happiness. That rare joy silenced all the noise that surrounded me. It was like time stopped.

His laugh pierced through the noise. The beauty, the rarity of it, arrested my attention. That's the effect of this second unveiling of the mystery in Ephesians. Its uniqueness stops people in their tracks. Diversity and unity can actually coexist in Christ. It is evidence of the supernatural. It is a powerful, potent picture of the mystery.

CHAPTER 7

When Jonahs Move To Jericho

Ephesians 2:11-12

NOVEMBER 9, 1989 - that is a date that will never be forgotten. It was the day the wall came down. The whole world paused to behold this history-altering moment. East Berlin and West Berlin, after years of segregation, finally met in peace. On that day the wall was abolished. Rendered powerless, it no longer had the authority that formerly isolated the two sides from one another. As a cultural force it crumbled. But the wall itself, as a structure, remained. What would happen to the structure? The world watched the days that followed as thousands of individuals visited that wall with sledgehammers. They began demolishing what had been abolished. Brick by brick, they tore down the symbol of their former division. These people were later labeled the "wall woodpeckers."

Ephesians 2 reveals sin as the wall behind all of our Berlin Walls. Sin created enmity between man and man. The cross of Christ not only ends the war but reaches further and brings peace. It's the cross that left the wall in shambles: Christ "put the hostility to death by [the cross]" (Ephesians 2:16b). The wall fell. In His dying, division died. As a dividing force, it crumbled. Christ has reopened the path to unity. The two have become one.

The Hostility That Ended Hostility

Paul mentions the cross as the instrument of peace in four different ways in Ephesians 2 (verses 13, 14b, 16a, 16b). Peace is the particular fruit of the cross. By the *blood* of Christ, Paul writes in verse 13, the far have been brought near. He tore down the dividing wall of hostility, reconciling the two into one body through the *cross* in verse 14. At the end of verse 14 and into 15, Paul writes, "In His *flesh*, He made of no effect the law . . . resulting in peace." Christ then reconciled the two into one by putting to death the enmity through the *cross* in verse 16. These terms: blood, cross (2x), and flesh all refer to this same event when Jesus died for sinners. His agony there brought an end to our animosity toward one another.

Do you see the mysterious irony? The cross, in all its brutality and hostility, became the instrument of peace. The hostility He endured calmed the hostility between us. God moves in mysterious ways. Christ's blood washed away our desire for blood.

The cross provides the peace, but it also opens up pathways into new dimensions of peace that have yet to be explored. The structures of our former hostilities, just like the Berlin Wall, still remain even though they have no power over us in the church. The cross removed sin's dividing power once and for all. But how do the remnants of our old hostility get hauled away? The answer: the cross. It also hauls away the structures of thought and behavior brick by brick, barbwire by barbwire. The cross is the sledgehammer that works to chip away at anything that threatens unity. The community that lives under the shadow of the peace-keeping cross refuses to settle for superficial ways of relating. They press in: giving the cross more and more room to expose their remaining sin and enable repentance so they can enter the fullness of the unity He purchased.

That's why Paul goes back to the cross when two believers in Philippi were bickering. He urges them to strive together by reacquainting them with the pride-expelling, unity-preserving cross of Jesus (Philippians 2:5-11). The church at Corinth was embarrassingly divisive. Lawsuits, critical spirits, judgmental attitudes, factions - you name it, it was there. How does Paul address these issues? He doesn't dive into them one by one at first. The Corinthians needed something else. They needed to recall the cross so he reminds them of it in Chapter 1 of 1 Corinthians. Why? The cross changes the atmosphere, giving humility a chance to produce unity again. Seeing the cross clearly serves as the antidote to lingering disunity in the church. It heals human relationships. It hauls away hostility.

The First Command in Ephesians: Remember

The Ephesians weren't immune to what was happening in Corinth and Philippi. They too seemed to be getting sidetracked from the cross. The structures of disunity that have yet to be hauled away are stubborn. The first command in the book comes, oddly enough, in Chapter 2:11-12 (emphasis mine):

> "So then, *remember* that at one time you were Gentiles in the flesh — called 'the uncircumcised' by those called 'the circumcised,' which is done in the flesh by human hands. At that time you were without the Messiah, excluded from the citizenship of Israel, and foreigners to the covenants of the promise, without hope and without God in the world."

Paul aims the command to "remember" at believing Gentiles. Paul urges them to never forget their life behind the wall. He takes them back, refreshing their memory of God's far-reaching grace. Why? Could it be that the "far" were now boasting of their late inclusion into the mystery? Could Jonah be living among them as well? Could the self-righteousness that drove him to despair be driving the Gentile Christians at Ephesus to feelings of superiority?

Could a fish be saving self-righteous Jonahs like us all? It can happen to all Christians. We turn mercy around. We get it backwards. It is not about us, and we have this awful tendency to forget this truth. We love to build our resumes. We stop living by grace and start living by comparison and self-righteousness. We keep others out while we go in. We leave some bricks untouched.

Remember, Paul urges in 2:11, that no one had any legitimate claim on mercy. If only the Jonahs in us all could remember his one moment of clarity when he declared, "Salvation is from the LORD!" (Jonah 2:9b)

Jonahs like us need to move to Jericho. Jericho, you will remember, is where God did the miraculous for the Israelites under Joshua's leadership. He tore down the wall that kept Israel from inheriting the land. Jericho's pride was humbled. Its boast rendered empty; its wall crumbled. Jonah needed his own Jericho moment. He needed his wall of self-righteousness to come down. This is what we all need if we are to enter into the fullness of the peace Christ has established.

Jonahs on the Inside

Looking back at 2:3, Paul had already smelled that fish that reminded him of Jonah among the believing Jews at Ephesus. He addressed this "brick" of self-righteousness that needed removing. He revisited their and his (since he was Jewish) former state outside of Christ. He wrote, "We too all previously lived among them in our fleshly desires, carrying out the inclinations of our flesh and thoughts, and we were by nature children under wrath as the others were also" (Ephesians 2:3).

Forgetting grace has the potential to re-erect the walls that formerly separated us. Something sinister lies in those old bricks that lie scattered around us. Sin lies in them. Sin can turn signs of grace into instruments of evil. This is evident in Ephesians 2:14-16, where Paul equates the "wall of hostility" with the "Law of commandments." This Law of commandments refers to the laws that God gave to Moses on Mount Sinai. It includes all the laws found in the first five books of the Bible. This Law was a gracious gift, but the sinful human heart turned it into a mirror of self-worth. Israel stumbled under this Law by using it as an avenue for résumé-building before God. It became the perfect platform for self-righteous boasting in the hands of the sinful human heart.

Paul knew the Jonah that lived inside well because he himself had Jonah-like tendencies. Paul's résumé was impressive: "blameless according the law" he writes in Philippians 3:6 (NASU). His obedience to the laws reinforced his self-rendered rightness with God. Or so he thought. His view of himself crumbled when he witnessed God's righteousness displayed on the cross. The cross shattered his résumé. He started viewing his former gains as losses because they kept him from Christ. Paul's internal Jonah had moved to Jericho and his wall came tumbling down.

This is what the cross does. It pops the balloon of inflated self-righteousness. The cross renders the gains of the flesh as loss. There's simply no room for boasting at the foot of the cross. "But as for me," Paul writes, "I will never boast about anything except the cross of our Lord Jesus Christ" (Galatians 6:14a).

Sin is given room to re-erect a pseudo-wall between us when these graces are forgotten. Gifts of grace actually can become mortar with a heart bent on self-righteous thinking. The church's oneness is found in Christ. Moving away from Him opens the possibility of new construction, or even better, old construction. Sin perverted the Law and can pervert grace into a divisive instrument.

Explore with me how self-righteousness threatens the unity Christ has established. For example, self-righteousness creates a culture of insecurity and comparison because the governing ethic becomes proving one's place with God and in the community. These Jonahs have a difficult time extending grace because they themselves do not live by grace. Those who trust their "sweetest frame" turn out to be not very sweet to be around. We like labeling some as deserving and others not. We hunt down evidence that reinforces our righteousness and other's unrighteousness. Debts against people who have offended us feel seductively reassuring. Their offenses justify our exclusion of them while reinforcing our sense of inclusion. Letting them in would threaten the core of what defines "us."

This premise is what kept Peter from eating with the outsiders in Galatians 2. It creates the "pity party" of the elder brother's anger when his father never threw a party for his obedience (Luke 15). That is why Jonah contemplated death when God refused to narrow His mercy to only those whom Jonah deemed worthy. Jonahs like us all turn mercies into mortar. The distinctions between mercy and merit become blurred. When our identity is misplaced, we displace others. Something in self-righteous people like the distinctions when two remain as two.

When I was writing this chapter, we were on a trip with my in-laws and our kids. We split the two older kids and the two younger kids between the two cars. As we ate lunch at Arby's, I overheard Emma and Owen talking about their secret handshake they had created. They showed Ben and Simeon. Immediately, what do Ben and Simeon do? They create their own version of their secret handshake. The lines were drawn. Two against two. There was no room to teach others, no effort to include the others.

We have our own secret handshakes, do we not? We set up false initiatory rites into our little community. We settle for so much less than God designed. These symbols of unity fall so short of the unity God ushers in through the mystery. The two become one in Christ. Our handshakes (sometimes our hazing!) run contrary to God's secret, the mystery, in Christ. The only way in and the only way to stay in is through Christ. The Spirit's presence among all who are in Christ secures everyone's full right to the inheritance. All who are in Christ have tickets to the party. God is not like us, creating barriers to getting on the inside. He has let the world in on His secret: Christ is for all peoples.

Jonahs on the Outside

But what if you are the one on the outside? What if your résumé has been destroyed by some sin or some glaring reason you shouldn't be included? What if you are the prodigal that has come home? Or the Ninevites who owned their wickedness? It may seem strange, but Jonah's mindset can be functioning among this group as well. Self-pity and self-loathing by the "have-nots" has its roots in self-righteousness too. A self-righteous person feels secure but an unrighteous person feels really insecure. We have felt this as well. Where do we turn? We either start repairing our image to regain our sense of worth or we give in to the despair of our unworthiness. Driven by this insecurity, we start a different kind of résumé-building.

Before his return home, the prodigal son prepared his confession to his father, seeking restoration as a slave because he felt too unworthy to be a son (Luke 15:18-19). He did not think grace could cover his sin and here comes that fish that saves the Jonah inside us again. He had bought in to his own exclusion, so he argued for his inclusion on mitigated terms. The overjoyed father's grace extends so quickly that the son can't even explain his idea to return as a servant (Luke 15:21). "No Father, I need to earn this," our inward Jonah pleads. This resignation to our own merited exclusion undermines the foundation of unity as well. When we feel that God and others can't or shouldn't love us based on our actions, we ignore the cross where acceptance is found. We accept the wall when Christ abolished it. We spread more mortar, but this time we are on the outside looking in.

Self-righteousness makes the community a courtroom where defense lawyers and the prosecution argue their case. The church becomes a context for criticism and suspicion. We throw bricks at one another or build them around ourselves. We need to hear the sound of the Judge's gavel that brings order and peace. It is the sound of the cross.

Not only are the bricks of our former hostility hauled away by the cross, nails are actually driven into our relationships that hold us together. We are loved in such a way that creates love for one another: "Therefore be imitators of God, as dearly loved children. And walk in love, as the Messiah also loved us and gave Himself for us, a sacrificial and fragrant offering to God" (Ephesians 5:1-2). How He loved transforms the way we love. Self-centered ways of living and thinking lose their appeal in the wake of such love. Chapter 2 of Ephesians is full of reminders for us as the church – reminders of where our lives would be without the cross. It is the cross that abolishes the wall and continues to take away each brick day-by-day, moment-by-moment, grace-by-grace.

The cross abolishes the enmity by silencing the boastful human heart. It breaks down the categories that divide us. The cross eliminates our ethnic pride or our feelings of cultural superiority. It stamps "unworthy" on all of our résumés and then surprisingly says we got the job because of Jesus. It emboldens the far to come near and exposes the nearness of the far. "He is our peace," says Paul in Ephesians 2:14a. The cross causes the arguments of the righteous to self-implode. It answers the guilty, woeful soul by lifting its eyes from its own filth to the only source of cleansing. "Come let us discuss this," the Lord argues, "Though your sins are like scarlet, they will be as white as snow" (Isaiah 1:18a). Jonahs need to *cross* over to Jericho and watch as the walls come down. An unimaginable unity waits. At the foot of the cross is where elder brothers and lost brothers party - together.

CHAPTER 8

The Mystery in Beast Mode

Ephesians 3:1-13

I AM FROM A SMALL town in northern North Carolina. We have a certain way of talking and relating that could perhaps make us a distinct people group within the American peoples. If I happen to run into someone from my hometown, we immediately start talking our "heart language." Other English speakers might find it hard to understand our lingo. Our subculture is wholly unique. Just ask my wife or keep reading this book and you will find out. One of those terms is the word "beasted." Growing up playing street basketball, if someone dunked on someone else, you might hear, "You just got beasted!" in the trash talk that ensues. The intended meaning would include something like this: "I bet you wish you were never born. You just got humiliated. Your every glory has just been stripped from you. Keep practicing, son, you gotta a long way to go."

I thought we had the copyright on this term until I heard the nickname of Seattle Seahawks' running back Marshawn Lynch. His running style has picked up this label: "beast mode." Lynch is able to shift gears to such a degree that instead of getting punished by the defense he starts inflicting the punishment. He gets hit and keeps running. It becomes impossible to bring him down. His mentality seems to shift from trying to go around people to running over people. When Lynch gets in beast mode, the opposition better watch out.

Ephesians 3 reveals that the mystery has shifted gears into "beast mode." All those who oppose it, watch out. It's busting out to every people group on the planet. The evil forces of heaven who try to tackle it do not stand a chance. The message to the cosmos is clear: you can't stop it.

Paul: Beasted by This Mystery

The mystery had broken through and picked up Paul along the way. For much of Paul's life, he was clueless to this story of which he was a part. But now, by a shocking reversal of God's grace, he finds himself playing a pivotal role. The one who once imprisoned Christians is now in prison as a Christian, all because this story opened a new way to view the world. And he is not despairing.

> "For this reason, I, Paul, the prisoner of Christ Jesus on behalf of you Gentiles – you have heard, haven't you, about the administration of God's grace that He gave to me for you? The mystery was made known to me by revelation, as I have briefly written above. By reading this you are able to understand my insight about the mystery of the Messiah. This was not made known to people in other generations as it is now revealed to His holy apostles and prophets by the Spirit: The Gentiles are coheirs, members of the same body, and partners of the promise in Christ Jesus through the gospel. I was made a servant of this gospel by the gift of God's grace that was given to me by the working of His power" (Ephesians 3:1-7).

Paul has been taken captive. He is physically in prison, but something else has him in chains. He sees himself as a "prisoner of Christ Jesus on behalf of you Gentiles." When Christ opened his eyes to behold the mystery, his own life became too small to preserve. He had to get the news out, no matter what the cost. Paul's life, Paul's glory, Paul's comfort – all of Paul - became secondary to the nations who needed to know. Their participation in this mystery enthralled his imagination and engaged his every effort. The good news was just too big to keep to himself.

What is the story that imprisoned Paul's ambition? It's the "mystery of the Messiah" that has now been unveiled. It's the good news that *the* Good News is for all people. All peoples, regardless of their race, culture, or history, can be included in God's gracious plan through Christ on the basis of faith alone. They do not have to divorce themselves from their cultural moorings to become a part of this promise. The gospel is hardwired to be embraced by all peoples. The categories of "near" and "far" have been eradicated by the reconciling power of Christ (Ephesians 2:14, 17). All can come as they are. Two polar opposites can both have access by the one Spirit to the Father. The mystery is that the good promises of God in Christ embrace all who come by faith: "The Gentiles are coheirs, members of the same body, and partners of the promise in Christ Jesus through the gospel" (Ephesians 3:6).

This news was new news to Paul. Previous generations were not let in on this part of the story either: "This was not made known to people in other generations as it is now revealed to His holy apostles and prophets by the Spirit" (Ephesians 3:5). Other generations had been given partial pictures of God's plan, but the breadth and scope of God's universal and multicultural plan were not fully disclosed. That God would bless the nations was clear to Abraham back in Genesis 12, yet *how* He would do that was not.

The means through which God would bless the nations He kept close to His heart until now. After the ascension of Jesus, the next move

God made was to enlist holy apostles and prophets by His Spirit who could unveil how He was now including the world in His blessing. God beasted Paul with this news: "The mystery was made known to me by revelation, as I have briefly written above. By reading this you are able to understand my insight about the mystery of the Messiah" (Ephesians 3:3-4). In other words, the Law would no longer be the means. Jewish culture would no longer be the prop. The non-Jews, the Gentiles, were now "in" on what God is doing, just as they are, if they are in Christ. They received the gift of full citizenship as God's people by virtue of their inclusion in Christ, not in the Jewish community. It's by grace, not by race. It's in Christ, not through the Law. God indwells all peoples who are in Christ through His Spirit.

God does not play favorites. He is not interested in racial profiling. The secret handshakes of old covenant rituals were never intended to keep people out. His grace is not capriciously selecting some cultures and not others. It is open and available to all through Jesus. The "incalculable riches" of Jesus cannot be exhausted by one culture and race. All can get in. He is a treasure chest full of enough wealth for the world. That kind of wealth simply has to be shared. The time was "now" for Paul. The wall that kept Paul's ambitions hemmed in had crumbled.

This "now-ness" of God's plan created a sense of urgency in Paul. The news was out! He knew he had not arrived at these massive conclusions on his own. This knowledge was a gift. He had to pass it on to others. To not pass it on would be to ignore the stewardship with which He had been entrusted. The message itself mandated proclamation:

> "This grace was given to me – the least of all the saints –
> to proclaim to the Gentiles the incalculable riches of the
> Messiah, and to shed light for all about the administration of
> the mystery hidden for ages in God who created all things"
> (Ephesians 3:8-9).

God's plan had been let out, and Paul could not keep it in. Now was the time for inviting others to peel back the curtain and behold the wondrous mystery. It is a grace to be able to proclaim this news of the "incalculable riches of the Messiah." It is a grace to be beasted by this news.

Prison could not dampen Paul's passion for the gospel of the mystery to reach every corner of creation. If we were in prison, even unjustly at that, I can imagine what would be on our hearts. "Urgent release! Pray for my freedom!" would fill our requests. Those desires are not bad; there are examples where safety and deliverance form Paul's requests (Romans 15, 2 Corinthians 1). But not here.

Paul's defiant tenacity to get the mystery out is revealed in his prayer request in Ephesians 6:19-20:

> "Pray also for me, that the message may be given to me when I open my mouth to make known with boldness the mystery of the gospel. For this I am an ambassador in chains. Pray that I might be bold enough in Him to speak as I should."

The original language of this letter, Greek, reveals a nuance as to why Paul felt he had to be bold. This verse would read something like this in a more literal translation: "I am an ambassador in chains for the sake of the gospel so that I might be bold enough in it to proclaim it as it demands." The bold claim that all are welcome in Christ finds its clearest expression in bold proclamation.

Notice the logic if we work backward through Paul's request. Paul needs God to do something, so he asks for prayer. What is it that Paul feels obligated to do? What "demand" is upon him as an ambassador? To make known the gospel. But not just in any way conceivable. The demand comes in that it must be proclaimed "with all openness." Open declaration befits the open gospel. The messenger and the message must match. A timid messenger when the mystery is in beast mode? No way. Paul knew his tone needed to correspond to the present force of the mystery. And this is something God must do for the messengers.

Bold, open proclamation fits God's open disclosure of the mystery. Paul's zeal for boldness stemmed from the bold claim of the gospel that all are welcome.

The gospel simply cannot be kept a secret. The mystery is out. A British theologian, Leslie Newbigin, nailed it when he titled his book *The Open Secret*. This gospel demands worldwide proclamation. It can't be stopped. It can't be contained to one people group. It breaks out. It must. The mystery is making its way across the earth.

Beasting the Earth

But the mystery has yet to advance into all the earth. The fullness has not yet reached its capacity. Hearing the good news is a prerequisite to believing the good news (Romans 10:9-15). People groups cannot believe if they have not heard. The Ephesians had heard and believed (Ephesians 1:12-14). Some groups in the first century had yet to hear. That's why Paul's ambitions stretched all the way to Spain where Christ had yet to be named (Romans 15:19-21).

The preaching of the gospel is the instrument by which God announces the inclusion of the Gentiles and ushers them into His blessings. This preaching is the way the mystery moves into beast mode on earth. The announcement of Christ's victory catches believers up in its peace-making dynamic.

The gospel's openness to all places an obligation upon all who have believed. Pauline-type servants are still needed today. Some who read this book need to consider the modern-day Spains of the world. There remain more than 7,000 people groups who have yet to hear of God's mystery. They remain in the dark when the lights have come on. They remain behind the veil when the veil has been removed. They don't have to stay there. Grace waits beyond the veil!

Who will peel back the curtain for them? Who will open the treasure chest so they can find the immeasurable wealth of God's grace in Christ? Will you? Is that your gospel-sized obligation? Have you been beasted, like Paul?

Paul did not expect all Christians to follow in his steps to the frontiers. But he did expect the global scope of the gospel to reshape the heart of all who believe. A global gospel produces global concern for the peoples who have yet to be brought in. He urged the church at Ephesus to join with him by praying for boldness and clarity when he proclaimed the mystery (Ephesians 6:19-20). Prayer precedes the light's penetration of the darkness. Prayer opens doors for the gospel. How is the gospel's universality reshaping your prayer life? Check out joshuaproject.net for a list of those who have to hear and watch as the global gospel enlarges your heart.

Paul invited some churches, like the church at Rome, to support his ministry through financial means. The early church took seriously this responsibility of taking the gospel to the unreached, and it affected their spending habits. Since the mystery will be unveiled to all, what better way to invest in eternity than to get involved? How are your finances being shaped by this global-sized gospel?

God has unveiled the mystery. Some still remain behind the veil - simply because someone has not told them. Who will tell them? Who will send those who go? Who will pray? The time is now. There is no room for procrastination and hesitancy. There is no more wondering what God's agenda is for the world. He has made it clear. The world is waiting.

Beasting Heaven

Before we unpack the rest of Chapter 3 of Ephesians, let's pause and make sure we are tracking with Paul as we read this text in view of the mystery. In Ephesians 1:9-11, God's mystery includes the reunion of heaven and earth in Jesus. God has given the world two parables — two heavenly truths dressed in earthly garb — through which to understand the unifying dynamic of the mystery. One verbal portal to the mystery is marriage. Marriage illustrates how two unite and become one (Ephesians 5:22-33). The church functions as the other parable to the mystery. In this invasion of grace, the future intrudes our present. Christ ends division and brings the two groups into one new man, the church (Ephesians 2:14-16). The church's unity evidences Christ's victorious, reconciling power at work in our age. She showcases the division-destroying power of the gospel. In Chapter 3, we meet Paul who writes this letter as one who has been enlisted to unveil this mystery through proclaiming the gospel. God's secret is out, and God sends out laborers who will push back the world's dark divisions with this light. This is a snapshot of Ephesians Chapters 1-3 through the lens of the mystery. God isn't finished announcing His mystery on earth until all peoples have heard.

God also has a message to heaven in Ephesians 3. Remember who dwells in the heavens in Ephesians? Angelic forces of evil dwell there while they work on earth (Ephesians 2:1-3, 6:12). These forces war against God's mystery, desperately trying to subvert God's program. They love it when two remain two. Satan himself watches for any opportunity he can get to slip in the door and undermine unity (Ephesians 4:26-27).

Listen in as Paul reveals how the mystery is beasting these heavenly forces:

> "This grace was given to me - the least of all the saints - to proclaim to the Gentiles the incalculable riches of the Messiah, and to shed light for all about the administration of the mystery hidden for ages in God who created all things.

This is so God's multi-faceted wisdom may now be made known through the church to the rulers and authorities in the heavens. This is according to His eternal purpose accomplished in the Messiah, Jesus our Lord" (3:8-11).

Notice that it is the church that reveals "God's multi-faceted wisdom" to the rulers and authorities in the heavens. What is it about the church that reveals God's wisdom?

The church reveals to these evil authorities that their scheming is over. Her presence alone demonstrates that God's wisdom has rendered their vaunted wisdom folly. Their doom is sure. Christ's triumph has taken their own forces and transformed them into His instruments of peace (Ephesians 2:1-10, 6:10-20). Their domain has become the trophy room of His grace as she displays His peace (Ephesians 2:11-22). When Christ ascended, their team and their turf were taken from them and turned against them. The message is clear: victory belongs to the Lord. God's program cannot be derailed. The mystery runs over all who want division to remain. This "beast mode" of the mystery enlists captives along the way.

The church keeps sending shockwaves through the heavenly hosts. With perplexing looks they reason together, "What happened?" "How did this happen?" Christ came, penetrated their forces, overcame their temptations, and rose from their most powerful weapon: death. They rushed to keep the news of His resurrection quiet but He ascended to glory, showing all of heaven and earth the war is over. God "appointed [Christ] as head over everything for the church, which is His body, the fullness of the One who fills all things in every way" (Ephesians 1:22b-23). Christ then magnifies His triumph by sharing His victory with those who believe. These believers are "seated with Him in the heavenlies" and united to one another on earth (Ephesians 2:6, 14-22). The heavenly hosts have been stripped of their glory. The evil forces have been overthrown.

In Michigan in 2009, a stunning ending to a high school football game caught national attention on ESPN. Plymouth was playing South Glen for South Glen's homecoming. Plymouth was up, 28 to 27, but facing the possibility of defeat at the last second when South Glen lined up to kick the winning 23-yard field goal. The whistle blew, and South Glen snapped the ball. The placeholder put the ball down. The kick was up. Blocked! Plymouth had won! The defense stormed to the sidelines, boasting that they had ruined homecoming, hopping up and down and hugging their coach. Their few fans erupted. The homecoming team remained on the field in shambles. They were crushed, dejected, and ashamed. They were so close to pulling out the victory. But then, out of nowhere, the video captures South Glen's coach racing down the sideline, screaming at his team to pick up the ball and run it into the end zone. The play wasn't dead! The referee hadn't blown the whistle! With Plymouth on the sidelines celebrating, South Glen picked up the ball and marched into the end zone untouched. South Glen won! One moment of triumph turned into a humiliating defeat. Plymouth could not believe it.

Plymouth and the heavenly forces in Ephesians must feel a lot alike. When the heavenly forces plotted together and crucified the Messiah, they thought they had secured the victory. It was over! They rushed to the sidelines, but the play wasn't dead. God raised Jesus from the dead and crowned Him the Lord of all. It was a bitter reversal for them to swallow. God used the very means by which they thought they had won against them. He placed Christ "far above every ruler and authority, power and dominion, and every title given, not only in this age but also in the one to come" (Ephesians 1:21). And His victory march marches on. God keeps raising the dead and seating them with Christ. Christ's stunning victory claims more and more. The church forms the ongoing announcement of His supremacy that brings the evil forces into open shame. Baffled in the dust, they witness the celebration on the other sideline.

From other passages in the New Testament, one can sense the frustration the church must be to the heavenly armies that oppose God. Satan may have a few small victories along the way, but ultimately, even these victories are turned into defeats. Satan tries to blow the whistle, sealing his mini-victories but Christ's resurrection means play is never dead. Christ holds the whistle. Christ's fullness fills the church (Ephesians 1:22-23). He makes these evil schemes implode on themselves, producing exactly the opposite of what the forces of evil desired. Christ reverses these presumptuous, momentary celebrations into platforms that reveal His glory, supply the church's good, and bring shame on these evil schemes. Christ turns the evil plots that were designed for the church's disgrace into means of grace.

These grace-reversals may have been the impetus behind Paul's words in Ephesians 3:13. There we read, "So then I ask you not to be discouraged over my afflictions on your behalf, for they are your glory." Paul's afflictions for the sake of spreading the gospel were numerous. Even this letter to the Ephesians was postmarked from prison.

So why would his sufferings lead to the their discouragement? The word for "discouragement" means to lose heart. Why would they be tempted to throw in the towel over Paul's afflictions? They might wonder if the opposition he faces will soon come knocking on their door. They might fear that all of Paul's talk of Christ's sovereignty was empty political jargon. Paul proclaimed Christ's victory over all from a prison cell? The mystery has shifted gears into "beast mode," but its Apostle remained in chains? Hmm. Something doesn't fit here. Inwardly, they may have felt this rising tension: either Paul is wrong or they are wrong for believing him.

Paul empathizes with the potential for discouragement, so he does not command them to change their mind in verse 13. He simply makes a request, "So then I ask you," he begins. There is no hint of a condescending tone here. He nudges them to consider a different view on his suffering. He wants them to reinterpret his sufferings on their behalf. His persecutions are not reasons for giving up. They actually become reasons for holding on. For Paul, his humiliation translated into victory for others. "They [his sufferings]," Paul writes, "are your glory" (Ephesians 3:13b).

Paul can talk this way because Christ's sufferings became glory for others. Christ's story opens the path to considering this reinterpretation. Humiliation became vindication. The cross, resurrection, and ascension of Jesus make Paul's request to exchange discouragement for glory both necessary and wise. Paul isn't putting a spin on anything. He is reading his story in light of Christ's and he wants the Ephesian believers to join him by adopting that vantage point. Christ's story forces us to reexamine our categories of suffering. Christ's death meant life for others, and Paul's "death" points others to Christ where they find life (2 Corinthians 4:12). It is no sign of defeat. It is a sign of Christ's victory, which is every believer's glory. Even the believers at Ephesus themselves had become partakers in this mystery, at least in part, through Paul's misery. Losing heart from Paul's sufferings would mean forgetting the pattern of Jesus' triumph: death then life. Suffering then glory.

Paul's opposition also pointed to another reason to glory. If he did not have opposition, one could assume he was no cause for concern for the other team. He was a non-factor. But opposition means the heavenly threat level has been raised. The opposition is a sign that the evil heavenly forces were scrambling to reclaim lost ground. The Ephesians can glory because Paul's imprisonment means enemy lines are falling. The mystery is beasting the heavenly host. They can only hope to contain it. But they can't. Their schemes keep imploding. God's wisdom keeps winning.

Three quick examples help us understand how God's wisdom nullifies the wisdom of those who oppose Him. Satan seized an opportunity to derail Paul in 2 Corinthians 12. Paul seemed like an easy target. Paul had seen the rare glory of the risen Jesus. Surely Paul will want to boast about that, Satan thought. Surely pride is knocking on the door of Paul's heart. So Satan enlists his "messenger" to go to Paul, kindle this pride, and bring out his boast. What happens? Christ actually enlists this "messenger of Satan" to engender humility in Paul (2 Corinthians 12:1-10). Paul begins boasting, not about his privileges but his weaknesses! I don't want to minimize that it hurt Paul to have this messenger. Paul prays for God to remove it three times. These reversals of grace may not be easy to endure. But one thing is sure: Satan strategizes against the church while Christ turns his strategies to serve the church. Christ employs Satan's messenger as a vehicle to display the sufficiency of grace.

Paul becomes so confident in these grace-reversals that at times he even employs them as his ministry strategy! We learn that Hymenaeus and Alexander had strayed from teaching sound doctrine in 1 Timothy 1:20. So what is Paul's strategy? "I have delivered them to Satan, so that they may be taught not to blaspheme." As a last measure, Paul banks on Christ's table-turning grace. Paul instructed the church at Corinth on how to deal with an unrepentant, immoral man in their midst: "turn that one over to Satan for the destruction of the flesh, so that his spirit may be saved in the Day of the Lord" (1 Corinthians 5:5). Satan schemes for destruction but Christ can turn them for salvation. Judas was not the end of Satan's list of strategic moves that came back to haunt him. It was just the beginning.

God's message through the church to the heavenly forces is clear: Christ's victory is secure. God's wisdom confounds theirs. His thoughts transcend theirs. Time is running out. The mystery is in beast mode.

Martin Luther captured Paul's desire for the readers of Ephesians well in the famous hymn, "A Mighty Fortress is Our God"[12]:

> And though this world,
> with devils filled,
> should threaten to undo us,

---

[12] Martin Luther, "A Mighty Fortress Is Our God," Written in 1529. Translated into English by Frederick Hedge, 1853.

We will not fear,
for God hath willed His truth to triumph through us:

The Prince of Darkness grim,
we tremble not for him;
His rage we can endure,
for lo, his doom is sure,
One little word shall fell him.

A little word. A little longer. That's all, church. The Right Man is on our side. He's all we need. No need to fear. We will not be ashamed.

CHAPTER 9

Unlocking the Mystery Through Prayer

Ephesians 1:17-23, 3:14-21

PAUL'S PRAYERS MAKE UP two large portions of this dense letter to the believers in Asia Minor: 1:17-23 and 3:14-21. Paul includes these prayers to show them the nature of his requests on their behalf. They also have another affect in the flow of Ephesians. Both prayers precede meditations on Christ's ascension to glory. Prayer, it seems, orients Paul to the limitless resources being funneled to the church through Christ's ascension. This becomes a model for us. A window is opened in prayer where Christ's authority and generous disposition toward the church can be beheld more clearly. This vision subsequently strengthens the church, filling her neediness with His abundance. Prayer unlocks the fullness of God in Christ through the Spirit so that the mystery's unity-creating, darkness-dispelling dynamic might be released into the community and through the community to the world. It is through prayer that the mystery takes flight in the church.

Let's read Paul's requests before we consider their impact on our reading of Ephesians and our lives:

"I pray that the God of our Lord Jesus Christ, the glorious Father, would give you a spirit of wisdom and revelation in the knowledge of Him. I pray that the perception of your mind may be enlightened so you may know what is the hope of His calling, what are the glorious riches of His inheritance among the saints, and what is the immeasurable greatness of His power to us who believe, according to the working of His vast strength. He demonstrated this power in the Messiah by raising Him from the dead and seating Him at His right hand in the heavens — far above every ruler and authority, power and dominion, and every title given, not only in this age but also in the one to come. And He put everything under His feet and appointed Him as head over everything for the church, which is His body, the fullness of the One who fills all things in every way" (Ephesians 1:17–23).

"For this reason I kneel before the Father from whom every family in heaven and on earth is named. I pray that He may grant you, according to the riches of His glory, to be strengthened with power in the inner man through His Spirit, and that the Messiah may dwell in your hearts through faith. I pray that you, being rooted and firmly established in love, may be able to comprehend with all the saints what is the length and width, height and depth of God's love, and to know the Messiah's love that surpasses knowledge, so you may be filled with all the fullness of God. Now to Him who is able to do above and beyond all that we ask or think according to the power that works in us— to Him be glory in the church and in Christ Jesus to all generations, forever and ever. Amen" (Ephesians 3:14–21).

Paul's requests basically revolve around God's agenda in the mystery. He never ventures far from the themes of unity, strength, and love. Prayer moves the mystery of the gospel from theory and knowledge to be fleshed out in practice and reality. It opens the door for the transition from the classroom to the lab, where Christ's fullness empowers our experience as the church. Prayer is the key that unlocks the treasure chest of Christ's resources available to the church.

This is why the "fullness" language of Ephesians fills the prayers of Paul. Sometimes he mentions "fullness" specifically and sometimes he just ushers us into Christ's fullness by lifting our eyes to Him. The prayer in Chapter 1 concludes with a sustained meditation on Christ's supremacy and sovereignty. This sovereignty energizes the church, not only has Christ risen from the dead and been given the Name above all names, He also is the "head over everything for the church, which is His body, the fullness of the One who fills all things in every way" (1:22b-23). The Ephesian believers are ushered to Christ's feet by Paul's prayerful meditation. They now sense it, feel it, and can be strengthened by it as Paul prays for that very thing (1:19a).

Paul's prayer in Chapter 3 asks God to impart the knowledge of "the Messiah's love that surpasses knowledge, so you may be filled with all the fullness of God" (3:19). He also prays that the "Messiah may dwell in your hearts through faith" (3:17). Prayer connects the resourcefulness of Christ's victory and absolute sovereignty with the needs in the church. God uses prayer as a channel of Christ's fullness to fill up what is lacking in the church. Prayerful congregations overflow with Christ's presence and grace. They manifest the mystery.

Just what was on Paul's heart for these believers? Several themes emerge. We will consider these as we unpack these prayers in two dimensions: 1) what Paul prays and 2) how Paul prays. We will begin looking at these requests under the heading "Praying to Know God." Knowing God has a transforming effect on our prayers so we will look at what shapes Paul's prayers in "Praying According to Who God Is" and "Praying According to God's Plan." This knowledge then transforms the way we see ourselves as the church so we will conclude with a section on "Praying to Know Ourselves."

Praying to Know God

The first recorded prayer in Ephesians starts with this request: "I pray that the God of our Lord Jesus Christ, the glorious Father, would give you a spirit of wisdom and revelation in the knowledge of Him" (1:17). Paul prays that God would grant them this Spirit-wrought knowledge of Himself. Prayer must precede this knowledge because only God can introduce Himself as He is to others. We don't arrive at good theology; we pray it down. It comes through the wisdom and revelation that the Spirit alone imparts. Paul wants God to be God to these believers. He wants the church to see Him in all His glory as the Father of our Lord Jesus Christ. Every member of the triune God is mentioned in this initial prayer in Chapter 1 because if He is to be known, He can only be known the way He is as the Father, the Lord Jesus, and the Holy Spirit.

And if we behold Him, we will become like Him. If we behold Him as He is, we cannot remain as we are. That's why Paul starts here.

Praying According to Who God Is

If we see God for who He is, our prayers must adapt accordingly. Paul's prayers in Ephesians have a certain rhythm to them: they ascend to God the Father through the Spirit and we are given an audience with Him because He is the Father of the Lord Jesus Christ in whom we have been adopted. Praying is a family affair. God is the Father of Jesus, and we are in Jesus through the Spirit who dwells in us. We can join Jesus in crying out, "Abba, Father."

Praying is communing with this triune God. All persons of the Living God are involved and active and present. The Spirit produces praying saints and ushers their prayers to glory. The Son gives them the right to be heard. The Father receives and grants the request according to the riches of His glory.

God's riches are made accessible through Paul's prayers for the Ephesian believers. This truth enlarges Paul's boldness in prayer. God's expansive glory expands Paul's requests. He prays big because God is big. God's vast ability inspires Paul to pray for impossibilities to become reality: "Now to Him who is able to do above and beyond all that we ask or think according to the power that works in us - to Him be glory in the church and in Christ Jesus to all generations, forever and ever" (3:20-21). Imaginations fall woefully short when God's greatness is in view. We cannot put a cap on Christ's fullness available through prayer.

Paul continues to transcend human categories when he prays they would "know the Messiah's love that surpasses knowledge" (Ephesians 3:19). Knowing the unknowable becomes somehow more possible through prayer. Formerly unknown dimensions of Christ's love become accessible on our knees. New strength is found as prayer opens our eyes to "what is the immeasurable greatness of His power to us who believe" (1:19). His power can't be measured. The incalculable riches of the Messiah produce incalculable requests. This God of unknowable love and immeasurable power has set His affection on the church and sends fresh resources for her good. This is why the "length and width, height and depth of God's love" pushes Paul's prayers beyond the edge of our imaginations (3:18).

Paul prayed with riches in mind: "I pray that He may grant you, according to the riches of His glory, to be strengthened . . ." Paul saw heaven's resources within reach when he bent the knee. If God were poor in love and weak in power, then tempered requests would be appropriate. We wouldn't want to burden Him too much. But that is not the God revealed in Ephesians. That is not the Father of our Lord Jesus Christ. To be "filled with all the fullness of God" (3:19b) becomes accessible through prayer.

Modesty gives way to confidence and boldness. With a God this grand and this gracious, what impossibility remains?

The fuel for Paul's prayers flowed from God's mighty power. He prayed to "Him who is able to do above and beyond all that we ask or think" (3:20). He prayed "according to the power that works in us" (3:20). He prayed that the church would be "strengthened with power in the inner man through His Spirit" and know the "immeasurable greatness of His power to us who believe, according to the working of His vast strength" (3:16b, 1:19). God is able. God's power makes the church able. The church finds strength as God flexes His arm through prayer.

Knowing God's nature and attributes transforms our prayers. His abilities open up new parameters for our prayers (if they remain at all!). A new world of possibilities becomes accessible on our knees. The church desperately needs to recapture a vision of who God is. A people who have seen God pray accordingly.

Praying According to God's Plan

Paul's praise in Chapter 1 generates the prayer that concludes Chapter 1. "This is why" marks the transition from the praise of 1:3-14 to the prayer of 1:15-23. Knowing God's program for the world (1:3-14) generates prayers that align with His purposes for the world (1:15-23). His program reshapes our prayers. Our prayers begin aligning with His plan. Praying results from being clued in to what God is up to in the world.

This sense of being "tuned in" generates the prayer of Chapter 3 as well. Again, Paul begins his prayer with "For this reason I kneel before the Father whom every family in heaven and on earth is named. I pray . . ." (3:14-16a) after he outlined God's plan through the mystery. The mystery's unveiling sends Paul to His knees. The open secret broadened the scope of Paul's prayers to include the world. He had "boldness and confident access" in Jesus because His requests aligned with God's purpose (Ephesians 3:12).

Understanding God's agenda for the world breathes new life into rote prayers and weary prayer-ers. Paul prayed, not merely out of a sense of obligation, but because his eyes were opened to God's massive plan. He was a "prisoner of the Lord Jesus" (Ephesians 3:1). Prayer becomes the reflex of the soul whose eyes have been opened to God's global vision.

Praying to Know Ourselves

Another aspect of Paul's prayers involves the church regrasping her identity as God's people and Christ's bride. She constantly needs to look in the mirror with Spirit-ual eyes. The church suffers from an identity crisis. It is a privilege beyond what flesh and blood can grasp to be the church in the world. If this self-knowledge was just a matter of looking in the mirror, why would Paul feel the need to pray for it? God must reintroduce the church to herself.

God needs to open the church's eyes to the "hope of His calling, what are the glorious riches of His inheritance among the saints. . ." (1:18b). The church is God's inheritance. Let's read that again: the church is God's inheritance. He redeemed her for Himself. She is His delight. The "hope of His calling" means her future is securely in His hands. It's rooted in eternity past and extends to eternity future because of the sealing work of the Holy Spirit (Ephesians 1:3-14). Her path leads to glory. "The glorious riches of His inheritance among the saints" means we are God's. God waits for the day when He will usher the church, in all her global diversity, to His fullness in her fullness. He sent Christ who died "to present the church to Himself in splendor, without spot or wrinkle or anything like that, but holy and blameless" (5:27). In a day when the church is tempted to look more and more like the world, it is good to remember we are not our own. We are His.

He waits to have us fully. To sum up Chapter 1's prayer: we need spiritual vision to understand that we are His, we are secure, and we are privileged.

The prayer in Chapter 3 adds this element: we are loved. Notice again the different ways that Paul points out that the church is loved in Ephesians 3:17b-19:

> "I pray that you, being rooted and firmly established in love, may be able to comprehend with all the saints what is the length and width, height and depth of God's love, and to know the Messiah's love that surpasses knowledge, so you may be filled with all the fullness of God."

The church is completely engulfed in love from every side. The church will never exhaust the riches of God's love, even when prayer arises to God to close the gap between what we understand and the real thing. The church never graduates from exploring new aspects of how He loves us.

But in this prayer, there is a means through which we explore these new realms of God's love. It is our love for one another. "Being rooted and firmly established in love" forms a channel through which we comprehend God's love and Christ's love (3:17b). Some churches content themselves with the shallow waters of God's love by staying shallow in their love to one another. They snorkel around, enjoying the views from the surface. Other churches put on the scuba gear. They explore the depths of God's love by diving deeper in their commitment to one another and in their tangible sacrifices for the good of one another. As they are prayerfully "being rooted and firmly established in love," their capacities to grasp God's love are expanded. The depths of God's love in Christ will be explored by us as we pray like Paul and venture deeper in our sacrifices for the good of others among us.

This "we" element is a key component to Paul's requests. That's why he mentions saints coming to grasp this love together. We experience this love in the inner man where Christ dwells through His Spirit (3:16b), but also together as "all the saints" (3:18). Some aspects of knowing God are reserved for all the saints, not just one saint. He is the "Father from whom every family in heaven and earth is named" (Ephesians 3:15). We press in to His love as we bend our knees together - in prayer and in service.

Church, when you look in the mirror, whom do you see? Do you sense the wonder which is you? You are God's. You are loved. You are secure. May God open your eyes to see your true identity.

Part 2: The Mystery Unleashed

CHAPTER 10

A New Sound of Music

Ephesians 4:1-3

PAUL HAS BEEN LET in on the mystery because God unveiled it to him. Paul accepted his role in this grand story and was playing his part by preaching the good news. Paul now urges us, if we are not following in his footsteps to the unreached, to begin playing our part. It is time for the mystery to be unleashed into the world through our corporate witness to its reconciling power. That is why Chapter 4 marks a major shift in the tone of the letter.

In the rest of the letter, Paul unpacks how this mystery plays out in everyday life. The focus shifts from exulting to exhorting, from unveiling to unleashing. Only one command - the command to remember in 2:11 - can be found in Chapters 1-3. But that is about to change. Chapters 4-6 jump from one command to the next as the mystery takes shape through the community that embodies it.

Listen for this change of tone in Ephesians 4:1-6:

> "Therefore, I, the prisoner for the Lord, urge you to walk worthy of the calling you have received, with all humility

and gentleness, with patience, accepting one another in love, diligently keeping the unity of the Spirit with the peace that binds us. There is one body and one Spirit – just as you were called to one hope at your calling – one Lord, one faith, one baptism, one God and Father of all, who is above all and through all and in all."

The rest of the book of Ephesians rests in the shadow of Chapter 4's opening plea to walk worthy. Life could not be the same after the secret was out. In the wake of God's revelation of the mystery, our ways of processing the world and walking in it need reprogramming. Walking worthy means we live our lives in step with Chapters 1-3. The first three chapters unveiled God's grand scheme. This brief summary of the mystery in chapters 1-3 shows why preserving unity is on Paul's heart when he began chapter 4.

1. Chapter 1: Unity wins over division in Christ. There is a moment to which (or Whom!) history hastens which will bring an end to our sad divisions. The universe, in all its fragmented mess, is moving toward wholeness in Jesus. Paradise lost will be paradise regained.

2. Chapter 2: A taste of this unity – this paradise - is available now, through faith in Christ and through the church. God reconciled former enemies when He created the "one new man" we call the church (2:15). This present peace foreshadows the coming peace when all things unite in Christ. In Christ, love has won, is winning, and will win over hatred and division.

3. Chapter 3: This mystery progresses onward through those who preach the good news like Paul. This news marches throughout the earth gaining more and more captives who have been enslaved to its reconciling power. The church is the thorn in

the flesh of the evil heavenly armies because God's wisdom has confounded theirs by her presence. The mystery advances to its climax. God's plan of restoration no longer remains in the dark or even in the background. It's playing out in our day and time. It's just a matter of time before heaven meets earth in perfect fullness.

What's at the core of walking worthy of this calling? It's the same core of the mystery: unity. The corporate life of the church must match the content of the mystery. That's what walking worthy means.

Notice how Paul begins with a "therefore" in 4:1, "Therefore I, the prisoner of the Lord, urge you to walk worthy of the calling you have received." "Therefore" means his charge is the outworking of chapters 1-3. The "calling" found there is immeasurable in its worth. By God's amazing grace, He lovingly designated us to be the recipients of His plan. We who were divided have been reconciled in Christ. We who were excluded have been mercifully included. This calling that began way back in eternity past ("before the foundation of the world") will carry into the coming ages where nothing but grace waits (1:4, 2:7). God's grace interrupted our fragmented lives and began picking up the pieces and mending our relationships. Walking worthy means walking in tune with God's grace-unveiling agenda for the world, the mystery.

Paul's word choice in 4:1 takes us back to chapter 2. Both chapters refer to the verb "to walk" as a way of life. The way we walked in chapter 2 was characterized by disobedience and wrath (2:1-3, 11-16). We ran against the grain of the mystery. We were agents of disunity and enmity in the world. The new walk outlined in chapter 4 has a new trajectory and a new purpose. We were at war and now we are called to walk in a completely different manner.

If that warring lifestyle opposed the mystery, what's it like to live worthy of our new identity? The answer? Keep the peace. Preserve the unity

(Ephesians 4:1-3). A life of loving unity with those whom Christ has conquered demonstrates our calling. Robust church unity unleashes the mystery of the gospel into the world with arresting clarity. Disunity confuses the message of the mystery. One writer summarized Paul's argument in the beginning of Chapter 4 well when he said, "The war is over so let us keep the peace."[13]

Have you ever heard an older hymn that's been musically altered in a way that doesn't match the meaning of the words? Your soul's expression is handicapped by the discord between the truth of the words and the music in your ears. A sorrowful hymn shouldn't be forced into a happy tune. It just doesn't work. Truth expressed alongside appropriate notes and rhythm draws out the soul to both think the truth *and* feel the truth. This is the way music should be. It should reinforce, accent, and draw out the lyrical truth expressed.

This is what the church should be as well. Its corporate life should reinforce, accent, and draw out the truth of the mystery. Too many churches handicap the world's vision of the mystery by keeping some of their former enmity around. Walking worthy means there is harmony between the mystery and our corporate life – our corporate rhythm. The content of the mystery is accurately "put to tune" in harmonious communities. Unity unleashes the mystery with full force. Paul's plea could be paraphrased in this way: "Showcase Christ's victory through maintaining the surprising unity which is you, church!"

A sociology professor at an elite American university skeptically began attending a church because he was interested in a young lady who was a member. As he visited and saw the relationships in the church, how they transcended class and racial distinctions, he was struck by the fact that he didn't know of any sociological categories that explained the phenomenon

---

[13] Gordon Fee, *God's Empowering Presence*, Baker Academic Press, 2009, pg. 701.

that was "them." Even with a doctorate in human relationships, his categories failed him. This unexplainable, unpredictable dynamic at work through that church's unity drew this man to consider Christ. Their strange unity at work opened his eyes to God's plan in the gospel to reconcile sinners. That church's music matched the message.

The Chords That Create Harmony

All good music is made up of the right keys and chords played at the right times. The right rhythm intermingled with the right individual chords – that's when harmony happens. Think of how tiny a guitarist's movements have to be in order to make the right chords. Calloused fingers in little places make all the difference. It's like that in the church. The path that accents the mystery doesn't start with a grand, miraculous act that leaves everyone speechless and in awe. It starts in the secret, hidden crevices of the heart. Walking worthy, i.e. displaying the mystery, begins by cultivating these heart attitudes: "with all humility and gentleness, with patience, accepting one another in love" (4:2). It's in the tiny movements of the heart that unity is kept safe.

These heart-chords protect the harmony that Christ has created among us. They have a unity-preserving effect. Conflict easily escalates and becomes divisive in the void of what Paul exhorts here: humility, gentleness, patience, and acceptance (which also carries within it forbearance). Without actively cultivating these postures of the heart, the very walls Christ tore down between us could be re-erected by our pride.

Have you ever noticed that most conflicts end up focusing on *how* we fight and not on *what* the issue was at hand? The issue is lost in the relational wreckage of the process. Humility, gentleness, patience, and forbearance take the "blows" in conflict and render them less damaging than they would be if pride, tempers, criticisms, and accusations were allowed to run free.

These four attributes of the heart have the potential to diffuse our conflicts and release the mystery at work among us.

Humility

The gospel itself creates this chord of humility in the heart. The structure of Ephesians starts with the gospel and what God has done for us and then moves to our responsibility and what we do for God. This is intentional on Paul's part because the first half of this letter to the Ephesians actually empowers what Paul commands in Chapters 4-6. Why did God orchestrate salvation to be by grace? "So that no one can boast" (2:9). Boasting-in-man and grace stand in stark contrast to one another. Humility is God's design in grace. He saved us in the particular way that most humbles us and brings the most glory to His free generosity. He brings us low as He exalts us in Christ. We are victors in Christ, yet our souls resist the triumphalism that creates pride. All because of grace.

One year on the day before Halloween, Bec's mom took our kids to Krispy Kreme. The kids carefully picked out the flavor and the spooky design they wanted for their icing. Ben picked the Ghostbusters theme. The minute I returned home, Ben ran to the van and told me he had gotten the "boast-busters" donut. "Boast-busters?" I said with a confused look. He corrected himself, but I still remember his name for that donut today. That donut reminded me of the gospel. God designed the gospel to be a boast-buster. It softens the prideful heart that makes us prone to division. "With all humility" is the first chord that preserves harmony. It is the fruit of grace.

Gentleness

Gentleness is the second "heart-chord" that preserves unity in Ephesians 4:2. Gentleness approaches others in tenderness and also responds to others with tenderness. A gentle person refuses to return the blow. He exhibits strength, not in repaying evil, but in absorbing evil without retaliation. This attribute, along with the others, has a shock-absorbing effect like the crumple zones in modern car engineering. In order to protect passengers from the impact of an incoming car, cars come equipped with "zones" that crush on either side of the passenger area. These areas absorb the blow so that the passengers are shielded from the jarring effect of an accident (within reason of course). That's what all of these heart attitudes do in a relational "wreck," especially gentleness. They prevent the relationship from suffering irreparable damage. They take the blows of harsh words, flaring tempers, and thoughtless critiques. The gospel creates crumple zones because the gospel puts us, as Jonathan Edwards wrote, "above the injuries of others."[14]

We have been more than accepted by the very One who has every right to criticize and condemn - we have been adopted into His family. The wealth of grace we have received from heaven crowds out the fear of not being liked on earth. That fear elicits anger when people threaten our core identity. But God's love, as it becomes the governing center of our identity, crowds out fear. We have a secure place in His family, which means our identity lies "above" the opinions of others. It's beyond their reach. Gentleness yields to the God who is our Defender. Their threats no longer threaten. We actually start looking through the mess, listening and learning from even the most unfounded critique. Knowing the blow won't ultimately harm us enables the ability to absorb the blow of hurtful words. The cross transforms our posture from defensiveness to gentleness. The issue at hand can be addressed without animosity and resentment. Apologies abound. In the grip of grace, we hold on to one another in gentleness.

---

[14] Jonathan Edwards, *Charity and Its Fruits*, The Banner of Truth Trust, 2005, pg. 86.

Patience

The gospel also enables us to take the long view with one another. The power to extend grace stems from the grace extending to us. We don't rush to judgment. Motives are given time to be revealed through actions and words. Suspiciousness is tempered by recognizing we all find ourselves in a life long process. We live at the crossroads of this mystery, occupying the space between what is and what will be. This "in-between" state keeps us patiently recognizing that we all have a long way to go.

Division comes unnaturally to Christians united by the Spirit. We expect change and hold each other accountable to change, but we know we don't govern the process. We can't rush the process. God does. The default posture of a patient spirit leans toward giving a lot of time for change in others and in ourselves. Pastor Ray Ortlund summarized what every church culture must cultivate well when he wrote: "gentle environments of gospel + safety + time."[15] A lot of gospel, a lot of safety for sinners to be changed amid acceptance without fear, and a lot of time for God to work among us – that's the new community God recreates through grace.

Forbearance and Acceptance in Love

Acceptance of one another is essentially an echo effect of God's acceptance of me. It is the reflex of God's peace-creating work in the human heart. Remember the elder brother in the story of the prodigal son (Luke 15)? He mistakenly assumed that acceptance had to be earned. He misunderstood grace and missed out on the party celebrating his brother's return. When we refuse to join the celebration that is the church – either by not accepting others or refusing to be accepted – we misunderstand grace. If we impose some condition for acceptance that must be met

---

[15] Ray Ortlund, The Gospel Coalition Blog, Posted on November 18, 2012.

before we accept one another, we deny our calling. We are at odds with the mystery. Paul wrote in Romans, "Therefore accept one another, just as the Messiah also accepted you, to the glory of God" (Romans 15:7). Grace-based acceptance showcases the division-destroying power of the gospel.

The Greek word for "acceptance" in Ephesians 4:2 also carries the connotation of tolerance or forbearance. Paul writes an addition to this heart chord in the words "in love." This orients Paul's intent toward the idea of forbearance. This meaning is represented in the footnote in the Holman Christian Standard edition of the Bible where the word "tolerance" is given as an alternate translation. Forbearance sees beyond the offense and accepts the offender. It diffuses the bomb. The gospel creates this layer of thick-skin that absorbs the blows that generally escalate conflict and drive division. But it's not callous-like thick skin. The gospel actually makes us more merciful and tender. We ourselves are well-acquainted with the sinfulness of our own hearts, so we choose empathy over bitterness. Forbearance stops the relational mess by changing the atmosphere. It is a way of neutralizing division with "preemptive forgiveness."[16] It gives room for God's grace to repair what is already broken.

In summary, it's a strange juxtaposition of heart attitudes that grace creates. It's thick-skinned forbearance mingled with compassionate tenderness. It absorbs the blow but stiffens at the same time so that the relationship won't break. Grace mingles intense accountability with unearned acceptance.

It's easy to read these words and agree in principle. It's easy to assume we are in tune and playing the right chords. But all of us probably need a retuning by taking an inventory of our hearts. It's time to do the hard thing and consider the actual relationships with actual people in our churches.

---

[16] Dave Harvey, *When Sinners Say "I Do": Discovering the Power of the Gospel for Marriage*, Shepherd Press, 2007, pg. 88.

What are your relationships like? Are we unleashing the mystery into the world or cloaking it through division? Does our music match the mystery? What are your heart attitudes toward _____ (you name the person)? Romans 12:18 gives us this exhortation: "If possible, on your part, live at peace with everyone."

The unity that God created in Christ requires diligence if it is to be pre-served. Paul concludes this section with a plea for us to reapply ourselves to unity with fresh diligence. He writes, "diligently keeping the unity of the Spirit with the peace that binds us" (4:3). Attentiveness to our relationships matters. Assuming oneness is dangerous. Relationships, if left alone, drift apart. The gospel will not preserve unattended relationships. Grace empowers us to attend to our unity and address potential threats to it. Grace creates peace-making activity not peace-assuming passivity. Grace creates sticky churches.[17] Do you need to take the first step with the one who offended you? Do you need to seek out one whom you offended? If the answer is "yes," Paul would urge us to not wait another minute. Walking worthy involves initiating tough conversations. It's worth it. The mystery is worth it.

"The hills are alive with the sound of music" became life-giving words to a world at war in *The Sound of Music*. A nun helped the von Trapp family and the whole world envision a new future by hearing a new sound - a new order of things that did not include war.

The world needs to hear the sound of music again. Unity is possible through the power of God to reconcile. Reimagining life beyond war happens through individuals in churches that let the gospel transform the chords at work in their hearts.

---

[17] I first heard this "sticky" concept from Larry Osborne's book entitled, *Sticky Teams: Keeping Your Leadership Team and Staff on the Same Page*, Zondervan. 2010.

CHAPTER 11

Remembering Our Roots

Ephesians 4:4-6

I N EPHESIANS 4:1-3, WALKING worthy involved cultivating the heart attitudes that preserve unity. These internal attitudes unleash the mystery by showcasing the gospel's unifying power. In Ephesians 4:4-6, Paul looks on the outside. What external reality binds us together as the church? It is none other than God in His trinitarian glory. His initiative and His activity among us all creates and sustains our unity.

Disunity usually results from over-prioritizing secondary issues, so Paul rehearses the core of our corporate identity in Ephesians 4:4-6. Christians share a common heritage; their togetherness shares the same root system. Like the massive redwoods in California that weather earthquakes and storms, the church's roots interlock. Some of the roots of redwoods are visible above ground. But beyond what the human eye can see is a whole network of interlocking roots that sustains their towering height. This underground togetherness, this subterranean inter-rootedness keeps them from falling. Paul stabilizes the church's unity by reminding her of her roots that reach beyond what the human eye can see in Ephesians 4:4-6.

Paul essentially reintroduces the church to her core self in Ephesians 4:4-6. If there ever was a theological "selfie" of the church, this may indeed be it: "There is one body and one Spirit - just as you were called to one hope at your calling - one Lord, one faith, one baptism, one God and Father of all, who is above all and through all and in all." Four of these roots remain above ground: one body, one faith, one baptism, and one hope. These experiences are assumed commonalities among all Christians. They are the visible signs that we belong to the same community.

But the other three go much deeper. If you dig a little underneath these visible experiences, a web of unbreakable togetherness appears. The church's roots intertwine with the triune God Himself: the one Spirit, the one Lord, and the one God and Father. Underneath each "one" of these four visible experiences of faith, baptism, etc. are the three persons of the "one" Godhead (one is repeated with every person!). Seven "ones" come together to give a sense of completeness: one body, one Spirit, one hope, one Lord, one faith, one baptism, and one God and Father. His oneness creates and sustains the one body. Keeping God's unity and His gracious activity before us is the antidote to letting our differences become divisive.

Let's consider the role of each person in the Godhead and their role in our unity from Ephesians 4:4-6.

One Spirit

On the heels of Paul's exhortation to diligently preserve the "unity of the Spirit" in 4:3, Paul begins his reminders of our oneness in verses 4-6 with the same emphasis. "There is one body and one Spirit - just as you were called to one hope at your calling" (4:4). We are one body through the Spirit; the body is because He dwells among us. Paul earlier stated, "You also are being built together for God's dwelling in the Spirit" (2:22). Receiving the Spirit led to the formation of the church in Acts Chapter 2. Paul reminded the divisive Corinthians, "For we were all baptized by one Spirit into one body - whether Jews or Greeks, whether slaves or free - and we were all made to drink of one Spirit" (1 Corinthians 12:13). It is our common experience of the one Spirit that makes our unity real and tangible. He births the body. The Spirit is not reserved for some and not others. There are not two tiers to Christian spirituality. We become one because we share His oneness. The Spirit also serves as the conductor that makes the orchestra of different instruments and different gifts play together in unison (1 Corinthians 12:1-12). This is why Paul mentions the one Spirit alongside the one body.

The Spirit is also linked to the "one hope of your calling" in 4:4. The one hope and one body are tethered back to the Spirit. The reason stems from how He makes the one body a reality through making us all partakers of the same promises. Our destinies are intertwined because we share the "promised Holy Spirit" (Ephesians 1:13b). His presence binds us to each other and to our common inheritance (1:12-14). His seal secures both present harmony and future glory.

One Lord

Paul digs deeper underground to find another root that binds the church together. We also share "one Lord, one faith, one baptism" (Ephesians 4:5). Both faith and baptism form the initiatory rites that signify our union with the one Lord. All of us believe on Him; all of us are baptized into Him. We all look to Him; we all live in Him. Passing through the same waters of baptism communicates our transfer from death to life in Christ. We are a new people, united under our common Lord, dead to the old things that divided us, resurrected to do life together.

It is so easy for church life to become "centered" on other things. Social justice, worship styles, theology, and methodology are good things if they are not made the center of our unity. If we begin revolving our corporate identity around these secondary passions, unity makes a subtle shift to our cause or our commonality and away from Christ. One method or one theologian does not have the gravitational force to hold us together. Only the one Lord can create and sustain diversity in unity.

One faith and one baptism bring us back to the beginning in order to refocus our unity on Jesus. He is the reason we signed up in faith and went through the symbolic waters of baptism that got us in the door of the body. If anything else becomes the mantra, the door to division is opening. Jesus must remain the explicit center of our corporate life. As the One Lord, He alone can hold us together as one: "For through Him we both have access by one Spirit to the Father" (Ephesians 2:18).

One God and Father

Paul then takes these shared experiences that are linked to the one Spirit and one Lord and digs even deeper into the character of God. The ultimate root that sustains church unity comes in verse 6: "one God and Father of all, who is above all and through all and in all." The "one body" with whom Paul started in verse 4 finds her true origin in the Architect and Administrator that brought her into being. The church is the Father's grand design. We are the Father's doing. He is the Source and the Sustainer of the church's common life and unity. Everything about the church begins and ends with Him, the One above all, through all, and in all: "From Him, and through Him, and to Him are all things" (Romans 11:36).

After surveying these massive commonalities that bind us together, it's hard to fight over the color of the carpet. It's hard to hold back forgiveness from someone who is the object of God's forgiveness. Bitterness, resentment, jealousy, and anger lose their appeal when we sense the magnitude of the Trinitarian Web that holds us together. Our tension becomes superficial in light of His activity and grace.

This is especially important in light of the mystery. The mystery unveiled means "Gentiles are coheirs, members of the same body, and partners of the promise in Christ Jesus through the gospel" (Ephesians 3:6). Our cultural rootedness is not uprooted by the gospel, which means Christ's value transcends personal or cultural preference. Our unity is not found in conformity to outward regulations or rituals but in the risen Christ. This means the church lives in creative freedom to be who she is as she is in the Spirit. We have been called in Christ communally, in our differences not from our differences.

Many hurdles must be overcome if diversity doesn't slowly drift toward division. This is hard work. It means that our narrow preferences cease to be the determiner of which relationships we deem worthy. It may mean that your church family looks a lot different from you and may not even be "fun" for you like hanging out with your peers. It may mean love becomes more of a labor prompted by God's Spirit than an overflow of outward similarities. In light of Ephesians 4:4-6, we sense the design behind all the diversity. We begin to trust the wisdom of the Father that brought us together. We remember the baptism that signified Christ's claim upon us. We sense the Spirit that indwells us and we are driven further together. We find a depth of unity formerly inaccessible to us because our unity now reaches deeper than superficial similarities.

Paul reminds us of what is of primary importance in Ephesians 4. What if our sphere of relationships centered around the triune God and those included in His redeeming activity? Our case for separating or transferring membership of our local church seemed pretty solid until Ephesians 4:4-6. Amen?[18]

---

[18] If the common core of Ephesians 4:1-6 isn't confessed and agreed upon at your church, it may be time to leave wisely and lovingly.

A. W. Tozer captured this centeredness that begets unity in *The Pursuit of God* when he wrote the following:

> "Has it ever occurred to you that one hundred pianos all tuned to the same fork are automatically tuned to each other? They are of one accord by being tuned, not to each other, but to another standard to which each one must individually bow. So one hundred worshipers met together, each one looking away to Christ, are in heart nearer to each other than they could possibly be, were they to become 'unity' conscious and turn their eyes away from God to strive for closer fellowship."[19]

Unity is the byproduct of "looking away to Christ." In Ephesians 4, Paul goes further than Tozer. He does not merely anchor our unity on Christ alone as the "tuning fork" but on every member of the triune God. He, in all His totality, makes the church, in all her diversity, beautifully and wonderfully - together.

A church that holds together despite every earthly reason not to testifies to the greatness of the mystery.

---

[19] A. W. Tozer, *The Pursuit of God*, A WLC Book, pg. 74.

CHAPTER 12

A Greenhouse Growing

Ephesians 4:7-16

OUR COLLEGE MINISTRY SIGNED up to tackle preparing and supplying the food for a community service event where thousands of people were expected. Part of our role was to keep everyone hydrated in the blistering summer heat of North Carolina. With all the humidity, any temperature above 90 degrees can be stifling. And on that day, it was expected to be in the 100s. We decided to partner with a church nearby where we could fill up our water coolers and bring them back to the site of the event.

The plan seemed good on paper. But it didn't go as smoothly as we had hoped. As expected, it was hot. Stinkin' hot. The lines began to form, and our water team started to work. Their first trip to the church, the church that was only a few blocks away on paper and a few minutes away by car, became a 10- to 15-minute trek. Why? A marathon happened to be taking place that day as well. Many of the streets in downtown Raleigh were closed. The longer route meant that our water coolers couldn't keep up with the need. As soon as the team returned with new water, the previous coolers were empty. Thousands of people were out in the heat, thirsty, sweaty, and everyone's stress level was rising. The plan seemed good before the event.

The church downtown had all the water we needed, but now the way was blocked.

That is not the case with the spiritual supply line from heaven for the church in Ephesians. Christ Jesus' ascension opened the path permanently for the church to have fresh supplies of heavenly resources. His fullness is always available and accessible to meet her need. That is the point of Ephesians 4:7-10:

> "Now grace was given to each one of us according to the measure of the Messiah's gift. For it says: When He ascended on high, He took prisoners into captivity; He gave gifts to people. But what does 'He ascended' mean except that He descended to the lower parts of the earth? The One who descended is also the One who ascended far above all the heavens, that He might fill all things."

The supply line remains permanently open by His journey to earth and His march back to heaven. No unforeseen circumstance can block the way. Jesus' incarnation and ascension secured both the resources and the means for the church to flourish.

Ephesians 4 highlights the watershed moment when He ascended into the heavens. First, He descended to enter the fray. The concept of "descending" shows us that the pre-existent Son, dwelling in the heavenly realm, took on flesh and descended to the earth. He took on His foes and defeated them at every turn, from the wilderness temptation to the weary garden of Gethsemane, to the cross where His enemies thought they had won. He was vindicated when He arose and ascended. He "ascended far above all the heavens, that He might fill all things" (4:10). There would be no unleashing of the mystery had this march through the heavens not happened.

Christ's fullness overflows to meet the church's every need.

Paul shows how Christ nourishes the church in 4:7 when he writes, "Grace was given to each one of us according to the measure of the Messiah's gift." To explain the Messiah's gift, Paul appeals to Psalm 68 in Ephesians 4:8: "When [Jesus] ascended on high, He took prisoners into captivity; He gave gifts to people" (Psalm 68:18). The ascension and the giving of gifts are linked. Christ distributes the spoils of His victory to every member of His body as spiritual gifts.

Notice too that this language of "giving" is picked up again in verse 11: "And He personally gave some to be apostles, some prophets, some evangelists, some pastors and teachers . . ." What did He give? He gave gifts to men and women and gifted men and women to the church. We are the spoils of Christ's triumph, uniquely gifted for the growth of the church.

The reigning Christ fills the church, not merely in a mystical union through His Spirit, but in tangible expressions of His love for her. She has the grace to grow because He supplies her with these fresh resources that flow from His throne. Ephesians Chapter 4:7-16 reveals how He constantly cares for her in how He fills her with His fullness.

One of the ways He cares for her is by washing her with the water of His word (Ephesians 5:25-27). The truth of the gospel transforms her and prepares her to meet Him one day in radiant glory. It makes sense that Christ would love her by sending her gifted men and women who can expose her to this truth. In Ephesians 4:11 Christ gives the church gifted teachers. He gave these roles to the church so that the church could know "the mystery of His will, according to His good pleasure that He planned in Him for the administration of the days of fulfillment" (1:9b-10a). Some of these gifted saints function to bring out into the light what God had hidden for ages past. Some of them were enlisted to disclose the mystery of God like the apostles. Today, some are used to initiate new groups that unleash this mystery (evangelists) and some to shepherd the church while teaching God's Word. The church taps into Christ's limitless resources by prayerfully heeding the Word of God taught by these gifted teachers. Christ exercises His generous headship by sending tokens of His love through teachers who impart the transforming truth of His Word.

Paul expresses the function of these teaching roles in 4:12-13. Christ gave them to the church for this purpose:

> "For the training of the saints in the work of the ministry,
> to build up the body of Christ, until we all reach unity in
> the faith and in the knowledge of God's Son, growing into
> a mature man with a stature measured by Christ's fullness."

Christ's victory took these gifted saints captive, employing them to unveil the mystery to the church. These servants are to train and equip the members of the body to use their gifts for the good of the body. They do not do the whole work of the ministry. They train and equip others to do the work of the ministry. They initiate the process of fitting every individual Christian into their Christ-given role to bless the church.

Why? What is the ultimate goal of everyone's participation in the process of ministry? The end goal is breathtaking in its scope. First, the process starts with the truth that begins its transforming work in the church. This transformation results in the church working together in service. This process edges the church closer and closer to the very fullness of Christ. The gap between the church's imperfection and her likeness to Christ is progressively shrinking. His fullness inches in to fill the holes that remain. Paul labels the end goal "the unity of the faith" and the "knowledge of God's Son" (Ephesians 4:13). This knowledge of God's Son, when attained, will mean that the wedding day has arrived. Until then, the Groom prepares the bride to be presented to Him in "splendor, without spot or wrinkle or anything like that, but holy and blameless" (Ephesians 5:27b).

Jesus is everything to the church and supplies everything for her. The church's growth began with Jesus' victorious ascension, moves forward by Jesus' empowering enablement, and moves toward Jesus' fullness for her complete enjoyment. His gifts prepare her for her greatest treasure: Himself. She waits and remains on earth but isn't confined to natural resources. However faint it may seem, a glimpse of heaven is available on earth through her corporate life.

Imagine the church as a kind of greenhouse for growth and at the same time a greenhouse that is growing. The church listens, grows, matures, feeds, and expands. She cannot remain stagnant or still. The Conqueror is on the move. The Groom is in pursuit. More and more people are brought as more and more fullness enters in.

Contrast the ever-renewing picture of the church in Ephesians 4 with the corruption at work in the fallen world in which we live (Romans 8). There we learn that the earth is held captive to decay until God removes the curse. The church in Ephesians is held captive to a different dynamic. Christ's ever-replenishing resources fuel her renewal: "He took prisoners into captivity and gave gifts to men" (Ephesians 4:8). Christ's new creation, the church, flourishes while the old creation decays.

This process of renewal and growth has a protective aspect to it. Verse 14 indicates that the church is not completely safe until she arrives at the goal of complete maturity and unhindered intimacy with Christ. Christ has opened a safe passage to His presence in Ephesians 4:7-13. In that path, Paul writes, "We will no longer be children, tossed by the waves and blown around by every wind of teaching, by human cunning with cleverness in the techniques of deceit" (4:14). The danger comes when we undermine the process by refusing to submit to truth or serve together. This danger of independence and indifference leaves us vulnerable. It cannot ultimately block the supply line, but it does indicate that we are entertaining other potential suppliers. This diversion keeps us immature, Paul notes, and we open ourselves to teaching that distracts us from Christ or is not centered on Christ. Human cunning takes us off the safe path. It restricts the supply line.

Like the light from a lighthouse that helps captains navigate rough waters and jagged coastlines, the light of truth guides us home. We will not be tossed by the waves and by every wind of teaching as we press on toward maturity, together. Discernment is needed because error does not usually boast of its incorrectness. It is cunning and crafty, just like that serpent that tempted Eve.

This false teaching prevents the church from growing into her fullness, "the unity of the faith" (4:13). It tosses her back and forth from one teaching to another, distancing her from the true Source of her growth. One of my friends used to work at a landscaping company. His company was managing many lawns and had tanker trucks filled with fertilizer, so they could handle the heavy load. One day his boss told him to transfer the chemicals from one truck to another that had some fertilizer but needed a little more. He obeyed and filled the tank that what was lacking with the other's fertilizer. About four weeks later, the owners of five different lawns called and complained because their green grass was now brown and wilted. Everything had died. Everything. Eventually they traced the source of these dead yards back to the truck with the mixed chemicals. Something about mixing the "fertilizer" killed everything it touched. The chemical and the truck looked right on the outside, but it ended up being poisonous and deadly.

If the church is the greenhouse, the fertilizer for her growth comes from those with teaching gifts who preach the right gospel. A mixture of truth and error undermines the growth of the church and can be deadly to her life. It can become poison instead of provision if it is not centered on Christ.

This speaking the truth isn't merely the teachers' role – it is the entire church's responsibility. In Ephesians 4:15, Paul continues outlining the safe passage to Christ's fullness when he writes, "But speaking the truth in love, let us grow in every way into Him who is the head - Christ." The environment of this greenhouse maintains its health by saturating it with truth. Gifted teachers rereveal the unveiled truth. Every member then reinforces the truth by rehearsing it together in love. The whole culture becomes truth-filled. Loving words of truth provide for the church's maturity. Truth crowds out the deceit and error that mixes the gospel with some phony substitute. All of us, as members of our local churches, have a responsibility to cultivate the truthful, loving environment that provides for our growth. God's Word, as writer and pastor Jonathan Leeman teaches, must "reverberate" among us.[20]

Christ's victory employs every member of the church to be a channel of blessing to the body: "From Him the whole body, fitted and knit together by every supporting ligament, promotes the growth of the body for building up itself in love by the proper working of each individual part" (Ephesians 4:16). Christ supplies her with good doctrine. Christ supplies her with the gift of one another. Christ supplies her with gifts for one another. She has all she needs in Him.

Ephesians 4 beckons us to be careful and to be faithful as the church. We must be faithful with our roles, faithful to speak the truth in love, and faithful to be equipped by the teachers that Christ has entrusted to the church. Together, we must deal gently and appropriately with error in our teaching and error in our practice. Truth instigates the process of correction and repentance that we weather together as the community. We sit under the Word in order to grow up into Him. Christ fills us so we venture further in our sanctification and deeper in our love for one another.

---

[20] Jonathan Leeman, *Reverberation: How God's Word Brings Light, Freedom, and Action to His People,* Moody Publishing Company. 2011.

Ephesians 4:4-6 outlines unity's foundation, and Ephesians 4:7-16 outlines unity's perfection. The church isn't merely about avoiding disunity and staying together for the sake of staying together. It is about something much bigger and grander. Christ didn't just create a people who stop fighting. His victory created a people who dive further and further - together - into the riches of His grace.

In normal Western wedding ceremonies, the father of the bride has the privilege of ushering his daughter down the aisle to meet her groom. Guests at the wedding honor that sacred moment by standing. The back doors open, and there she is – the bride, in all her spotless and radiant beauty, being guided by her father to be given to the groom who waits. It is a symbolic walk that encapsulates her life up until this point. The groom takes her from that moment forward.

Now, consider another context for that scene. In your mind see the doors open but not inside a church building but to a war. Envision that father, shielding his daughter in the middle of a battlefield with bullets flying, bombs exploding, and fear gripping everyone. If the church is the bride, that walk down the dangerous aisle is a picture of this present age. There are no safe confines of a pristine wedding ceremony. Enjoying the unhindered union that waits at the end of the aisle will require safely navigating this battle zone. This war may play out physically through persecutions but it also involves the mind and heart. It is a battle between truth and error.

Christ has entrusted this sacred task of ushering the church safely through this battlefield to all of us – teachers and members alike. The teaching responsibility of these gifted saints and the corporate responsibility to speak the truth in love enables the church to safely navigate the dangerous terrain between engagement and the fullness of marriage. The Groom's fullness awaits her. Persevering will be difficult. It's hard to submit to the truth, repentance is costly, and it's tough to speak the truth in love. Genuine relationships where we don't hide behind our sin take courage and endurance, but it's worth it. *He* will be worth it.

CHAPTER 13

Freedom from Self

Ephesians 4:17-24

ICHARD WURMBRAND, A PASTOR who died in 2001, suffered much for the glory of Christ at the hands of Romanian communists. He endured 14 years of imprisonment and countless beatings at the hands of those who oppressed him. But God's word could not be bound. In the midst of all the suffering, God opened the door for him to declare the gospel to many cellmates and even to the guards that tortured him.

Grecu, an atheistic lieutenant that had been responsible for some of Wurmbrand's pain, was one of the guards that heard the good news. As they talked one day, Wurmbrand expressed his love for Grecu despite everything he had done. Grecu was shocked. "Mr. Wurmbrand, why do you say you love me? I couldn't love someone who shut me up for years alone, who starved me and beat me," he replied. To which Wurmbrand answered:

> "When I became a Christian it was as if I had been reborn, with a new character that was full of love. Just as only water can flow from a spring, so only love can come from a loving heart."[21]

In the face of such love, Grecu too became reborn and a spring of love also opened in his heart. Wurmbrand noted how soon after his conversion, Grecu "bravely helped prisoners as best he could, through difficulties and dangers."[22] For a while he tried to walk the "party-line" by staying true to the communist party as well as his newfound identity as a Christian, but it didn't last long.

One day Grecu totally disappeared. Wurmbrand soberly reflected on this incident with these words: "to hide a true conversion is not easy."[23] Conversion resists concealment. That degree of transformation must come out. A heart so loved cannot help but love, even when love puts one in danger.

Wurmbrand's comment on conversion echoes Paul's point in Ephesians 4:17-24. True conversion results in a thousand little conversions that find expression through acts of love. One particular facet of this transformation happens in the mindset of the believer. A new way of thinking has interrupted the old. A "spring of love" has been opened that cannot be contained.

Paul begins this section in verse 17, "Therefore, I say this and testify in the Lord: You should no longer walk as the Gentiles walk, in the futility of their thoughts." This "therefore" connects the previous section to the current discussion. The truth of the gospel reprograms the way we think about God, ourselves, and the world.

---

[21] Richard Wurmbrand, *In God's Underground*, Living Sacrifice Book Company, January 10, 2011. Kindle Edition. Location 856.

[22] Richard Wurmbrand, 876.

[23] Richard Wurmbrand, 876.

God has already mapped out the direction of this new walk by His grace. The power to walk comes from God and the path before us has been opened by God: "For we are His creation, created in Christ Jesus for good works, which God prepared ahead of time so that we should walk in them" (Ephesians 2:10). The footprints of God's grace have gone before us. Good works are merely stepping into the paths of life He has charted before us. Paul urges us to no longer live as if we were still behind the veil - still walking in darkness - in Ephesians 4:17-24. We can't go back. We've come to far. It's hard to conceal a true conversion because it's hard to turn back on such grace, such love.

Life Under the Fence: The Old Way of Thinking

In 4:17-24, Paul contrasts two opposing ways to live. The differences that separate these lifestyles are rooted in the opposing ways these two groups of humanity think. One accords with Christ; the other opposes Christ. One unleashes the mystery; the other suppresses it. One fits the new self; the other fits the old.

In Ephesians 4:17-22, Paul describes the mental state of those who are outside of Christ like this: "the futility of their thoughts," "darkened in their understanding," and "excluded from the life of God, because of the ignorance that is in them and because of the hardness of their hearts." This hardness is a result of callousness: "They became callous and gave themselves over to promiscuity for the practice of every kind of impurity with a desire for more and more" (4:19). Paul's blanket summary in verse 22 captures the decay at work in this mentality when he writes that the old self "is corrupted by deceitful desires."

Paul is out to refresh our memory so that we might taste how bitter our rebellion really was. It was a sad state of being, a hard life. Dark, deceitful, unsatisfying - this cyclical way of thinking engrosses the unbelieving mind as it fails to produce what it promises. Over and over again this mindset comes up empty and this emptiness creates more room for more emptiness. This futile cycle perpetuates itself because the objects of their desires cannot satisfy. He or she experiments with "every kind of impurity" because one kind never fully fulfills the desire (4:19b). The people who dwell in this world of thought hop from pleasure to pleasure, always searching but never finding. They wander in the dark (which they think is light), "excluded from the life of God" (4:18b). This broken way of thinking inevitably leads to broken lives and broken relationships.

What is the center of this old way of thinking? Self. This mindset focuses on self and its needs and uses others to meet those perceived needs. Self is king and this king is greedy. "What I want" governs every decision. "Me" shapes the "we." But one huge problem confronts this way of thinking: it is inherently self-defeating. Self is an insatiable master. No slave can meet the demands of self, thus lasting satisfaction eludes its grasp. The slaves that self employs to produce satisfaction or protection are actually functional saviors, idols of our own making. They either fulfill us and we become so attached to them that we cannot break free (who is serving whom?) or they disappoint us so that we angrily choose another. Either way we end up enslaved or searching for another slave. We dwell in the dungeon of our own deceitful desires.

This way of thinking does not lead to renewal, wholeness, or satisfaction because our chosen savior is not able to handle the weight we have placed upon it. We have formed an idol and after serving it (which ironically feels like we are enlisting it in our service), we end up resembling its image. "Those who make them are just like them," the psalmist declared in Psalm 115. The point is that idols, i.e. functional saviors, only leave us empty just as they are empty. This is the folly of idolatry. This mindset walks around in the dark, inhabiting a self-conceived world full of self-centered desires and self-designated saviors. A door out of this dungeon only leads to another grungy cell. The process hollows out our very capacity for true joy. God is nowhere to be found in that world of thought.

It was fourth grade and it was snowing – like I had never seen before. My friend, Rob, and I headed out to go exploring. The snow kept coming and coming. Hours later, we ended up at a baseball field. The field was surrounded by a fence and the sun was beginning to set. Cold and wet, we didn't want to walk the path that would have taken us all the way back around the field to get home, so we decided to make it easier. We would climb the fence. Only one problem: three layers of barbed wire on top of the fence stood in our way.

Rob, who was dressed in his thick ski pants and winter jacket, went first. He almost made it over the third layer of barbwire when his weight shifted and he lost his grip. The barbwire ripped into his jacket and ski pants, leaving him dangling in the air by hundreds of tiny little threads of cotton. I had to help, but I couldn't climb over because the fence would shake, sending him into the thorn bushes below. I couldn't go around the field because that would take too long.

I looked around and then remembered a hole between the ground and the fence not too far away. On summer nights, we would slither through this hole in order to get into baseball games. I laid down and tried to body crawl through it. But because of the thickness of the snow and my own winter jacket, my neck became trapped under the fence. The fence had dug into my neck, so I couldn't go backward or forward. I couldn't even get the right angle with my hands in order to dig out of the snow. I was stuck with my chin buried in the snow.

While he was suspended in the air and I was lying facedown in the ground, we were calling for help. The minutes seemed go by like hours. Suddenly, I heard a rip and a pop, the cotton strings gave way, and there Rob went, tumbling right into the thorn bushes below. He came to me but wasn't strong enough to pull the fence back, so he ran and got his mom. She was able to work the fence enough to loosen my neck. We were free! With frostbite and bruises, we headed home. It was such a relief to change from those stiff, wet clothes to dry ones. We sat near the fire to thaw out. Warm air had never felt so good.

What seemed like the easy way home ended up being much more difficult. This childhood experience parallels the life excluded from God. We get in a jam and take the easy way; we choose a path or a "savior" and then we end up getting stuck in the process. The fence we choose to climb becomes the fence that leaves us ashamed in the snow. Then the cold takes over, and we become numb to the hurt we inflict on others and even on ourselves. We are stuck under the fence. We feel chained to our empty selves.

The lights have come on for those who are in Christ so that they see the futility of this way of living. The hollowness of these paths and these "saviors" have been exposed. Our hearts have been softened to see the damaging effects of sin. It hurts others. It hurts us. This is why Paul urges us to keep our distance from our former manner of life (Ephesians 4:17). We would only entertain those thoughts if we had forgotten how futile and cold that way of life really was. We no longer live excluded from the One True God so how could we go back?

Life Beyond the Fence: A New Way of Thinking

There is a new way home. Paul outlines how the old path had nothing in common with this new way. He writes, "But that is not how you learned about the Messiah" in Ephesians 4:20a. We can get beyond the fence of our self-centered mindset in a way that does not leave us humiliated, cold, and screaming for help.

The Messiah is not an idol of our creation. He is the Lord of all. He is able to provide what He promises. His fullness breaks the cycle of emptiness. We did not stumble upon Him in the darkness of deceit. Charles Wesley reflected on that moment when Christ diffused a "quickening ray" to his heart like this: "I woke, the dungeon flamed with light! My chains fell off, my heart was free."[24] Paul describes that moment as Jesus bringing His truth home to our hearts, when "you heard about Him and were taught by Him, because the truth is in Jesus" (4:21). The truth of Jesus opens our hearts and opens the path home. We are free to live and love. Regarding this newfound freedom, David Wells wrote:

> "The emancipation that the Gospel offers, after all, is not only from the judgment of God but from the tyranny of self as well. Its freedom is, in part, the freedom to be forgetful of the self in its imperious demands and its insatiable appetite for attention, the freedom to think that God is important in and of Himself and not simply in relation to what He can do for us."[25]

Jesus delivers us from the tyrant who is us! Freedom from self, freedom from false saviors and vain hopes – that's the redemption Christ provides. No more fences to climb. No more being left out in the cold. No more dark dungeons.

Life beyond the fence became possible when Jesus became the center: "You took off the former way of life, the old self that is corrupted by deceitful desires; you are being renewed in the spirit of your minds; you put on the new self, the one created according to God's likeness in righteousness and purity of the truth" (Ephesians 4:22-24). This de-clothing of our old self-centered self by Christ renews the soul by renewing the mind. Conversion is indeed hard to conceal because it leads to a continual overhauling and renewing of the entirety of our lives. God's goodness and warmth draw us home to Him. This warmth from Him creates people who have warm relationships of wholeness and purity. It's not about us anymore.

---

[24] Charles Wesley, "And Can It Be That I Should Gain," *Psalms and Hymns,* 1738.

[25] David Wells, *Losing Our Virtue,* Wm. B. Eerdmans, 1998, pg. 204.

Repentance, a word for having a change of mindset, feels right. It is the taking off of the wet clothes and exchanging them for the dry ones. We were "excluded from God," but now we are becoming like God. This feels right because our hearts are restless until they rest in God.[26] This way is life-giving and liberating. It leads us home to sit by the fire where our numbness departs and true feeling returns. This overhaul, this recreation leads to true freedom that empowers genuine love.

This new way stands in stark contrast to the former way. "In righteousness and purity of the truth" takes the place of impurity, promiscuity, and corruption (Ephesians 4:24b). The mindset of the new self reshapes people who begin resembling the very likeness of God. Righteousness transforms their relationships. They become trustworthy. They have integrity. They do not leave others insecure. They keep their word. Purity characterizes their intentions. Self isn't enlisting slaves but now submits itself in the service of others. Pure in motive, pure in heart, pure in passion, they breathe fresh life into relationships.

Remember Grecu? His old life was exchanged for a new one. He went from inflicting harm on the prisoners to enduring harm for the sake of the prisoners. A hardened man had turned into a humble servant. The irony is that before being converted, he thought he was "free" and Wurmbrand was imprisoned. He came to realize it was just the opposite. He was enslaved and Wurmbrand was free all along. No prison can confine the soul that is freed from self and freed to love in Christ.

---

[26] St. Augustine, *Confession*, Oxford University Press, 2008, pg. 3.

CHAPTER 14

Sticky Ethics for a Sticky Community

Ephesians 4:25-32

I STILL REMEMBER MY COACH'S face. We had a chance to win it all. Of all the high school teams in our area, we had the talent to take home the trophy. The state championship seemed within our reach. But around the middle of our season, things started unraveling. We started being lazy at practice. Christmas break gave us a week off of practice and we returned unfocused and unmotivated. After two of our best players missed the bus for an away game that we ended up losing, coach held an emergency team meeting at practice the next morning. We sat in a circle around our high school's emblem and coach took us back through our high school's history. He told us about the trophy that could be ours if we wanted it enough. He called us out as individuals where he thought we were putting other things before the team. It was sobering. We needed to re-examine our priorities. It was time to put the "we" before the "me."

We obviously did not want it enough. We ended up losing in the second round of the state playoffs that year even though we had the talent. The problem was that the championship trophy did not have the power to change our priorities. It wasn't compelling enough to change what we valued at the time. That team meeting had no permanent effect on us. It would have taken a miracle for a bunch of teenagers to see beyond themselves to the team. We didn't, and so we lost.

The gospel is just that kind of miracle. It creates a people in whom the "me" is subjected to the "we." The first displacement of self from the center for Christ leads to a further displacement of self for the community. We used to belong to communities based on how well the group served our interests. Not anymore. The gospel introduces a whole new way of belonging where the community comes first. This heart change manifests the depth of change made possible by the mystery.

Watch this new way of belonging unfold in Ephesians 4:25-32:

> "Since you put away lying, Speak the truth, each one to his neighbor, because we are members of one another. Be angry and do not sin. Don't let the sun go do down on your anger, and don't give the Devil an opportunity. The thief must no longer steal. Instead, he must do honest work with his own hands, so that he has something to share with anyone in need. No foul language is to come from your mouth, but only what is good for building up someone in need, so that it gives grace to those who hear. And don't grieve God's Holy Spirit. You were sealed in Him for the day of redemption. All bitterness, anger and wrath, shouting and slander must be removed from you, along with all malice. And be kind and compassionate to one another, just as God also forgave you in Christ."

Having Jesus at the center inevitably leads to another change of heart. Now self moves further down the list and becomes a servant to this new community. Jesus reprograms the heart to put "we" before "me." Belonging to this new community begins governing the way we behave. A new ethical process and journey has begun. Believing in Jesus leads to belonging to His body in such a robust way that the belonging itself begins shaping behavior.

Look for how belonging alters behavior in these verses. Ask "why" of these three verses in this section and watch this new corporate vantage point for ethics appear:

- Why put away lying? "Because we are members of one another" (verse 25).

- Why must the thief work and no longer steal? "So that he has something to share with anyone in need" (verse 28).

- Why be careful with what proceeds from our mouths? Because it needs to be "good for building up someone in need, so that it gives grace to those who hear" (verse 29).

Paul expects a massive change to happen in the depth of our hearts because of the gospel. Those who regard each other's interests above their individual desires are truly walking worthy of the calling. The community benefits from the security of truth-telling relationships, the fruit of the labor of their hands, and the blessing of gracious, timely words from their mouths.

The change even reaches their hearts. Paul writes, "All bitterness, anger and wrath, shouting and slander must be removed from you, along with all malice. And be kind and compassionate to one another, forgiving one another, just as God also forgave you in Christ" (Ephesians 4:31-32). Even in their hearts, they have stopped warring against each other and instead, fight against bitterness and anger that threaten their relationships. Malice has been choked about by their high view of membership. Sin is not given room to fester into bitterness as they take these attitudes quickly to the cross. Those who adopt this ethical process show the world the beauty of God's program in the mystery. They get it; they protect and preserve the oneness in the church who is a foretaste of heaven.

Questions like these shape their behavior: "How are my actions affecting the community?" "What burdens am I placing on the community?" "Am I being a blessing to the community?" "Are there ways I am acting inconsistently, like lying, with my identity as a member of Jesus' body?" There is a new "we" impulse at work in their heart. The functional core of their thinking that used to be themselves has been vacated and the church has moved in. This kind of thinking has a way of seeping in to all areas of our lives. Our ethics are transformed by our unity and our unity is continually transformed by our transforming ethics.

A Forgiving Community

This new community is not perfect. We will fail each other. We don't always consider each other's interests above our own. We haven't reached the full stature of Christ's fullness. We are a work in progress. Maintaining unity will not always be easy. It will have to overcome gross sin and evil malice at times. That is why Paul concludes Ephesians 4:25-32 with this verse: "And be kind and compassionate to one another, forgiving one another, just as God also forgave you in Christ." God forgave sinners at the cross where Jesus died. Paul revisits this moment because communities marked by forgiveness extend grace to one another just as God did. The old self responded in kind. You shout at me, I shout back. You accuse me, I accuse you. You slander me, I slander you. Not anymore. God's grace has revealed a different way of relating. We no longer need to protect ourselves or be proven right. We diffuse tension that threatens unity with kindness, compassion, and forgiveness. We can change the relational atmosphere by canceling debts and initiating healing. All because this is what God has done with us.

Forgiveness takes the blow for the sake of the team. It cleans up one spill at a time.[27] It does not add to the relational mess. The pursuit of justice or winning an argument has lost its appeal in the shadows of Christ who laid down His rights in the pursuit of reconciliation. Forgiveness does not keep the offender at arm's length or locked up in a cold, relational prison to make him or her feel worse. It closes the distance. It unlocks the cell. It initiates the embrace.

But for those who know the pain of being hurt by brothers and sisters in Christ, this is really hard. Oneness lost is not easily regained. There is a cost. That is why Paul closes Chapter 4 with this empowering reminder to forgive "one another, just as God also forgave you in Christ." God-like saints forgive in God-like ways. The cross expels bitterness because there we see the God who closed the gap. There we see Christ who absorbed the blow. God refused to return evil for evil and canceled the debt against us. In like fashion, we are to extend grace to all.

A Truthful Community

Truth fills the community that reflects the mystery. It cannot live the lie and walk in the dark any longer: "Since you put away lying, speak the truth, because we are members of one another" (4:25). Lying loses its lure in light of the truth found in Jesus. We are now one with one another so we live as open books, not hiding or covering who we are or what we have done. We welcome the exposing light that is coupled with sufficient grace. We no longer need to manipulate people to serve us or think more highly of us by lying. We treat others how we would want to be treated because we are bound together as members of one body. The paralyzing fear of disappointing others has been stripped of its power over us because we have already been forgiven for the grossest disappointment possible in our rebellion toward God.

---

[27] Dave Harvey, *When Sinners Say I Do*, page unknown.

We are not members of this body because we deserved it based on our performance. It's all by grace. This grace enables telling the truth even when it's hard because the reward outweighs the risk. We are members of the one body. Truth reinforces and protects that bond. Truth-telling is characteristic of a community that has been gripped by God's open secret.

An Angry Community

Paul addresses another attitude that ironically unleashes the mystery: anger. In Ephesians 4:26-27, he says, "Be angry and do not sin. Don't let the sun go down on your anger, and don't give the Devil an opportunity." This exhortation to be angry is a partial quotation from Psalm 4. The psalmist, David, finds himself suffering injustice when he issues the command to himself and others listening to be angry and yet not sin. Anger, in this case, is the appropriate response to injustice. Paul exhorts the church, like David exhorted those who heard him, to be angry and yet not sin.

This anger seems to be at odds with God's peacemaking endeavor through the mystery. It's actually not. If we lose our anger at what is wrong in the world, we lose our moral backbone. We don't understand the mystery. We forget who we are. Those who belong to the church are charged to keep their anger while also being reminded to not allow their anger to go unchecked. "And do not sin" is key (Psalm 4:4).

There is another anger that threatens unity in Chapter 4 of Ephesians. Paul tells us to put off this sinful anger in verse 32. This is not the anger David advocates for in Psalm 4. It is a corrupted version of the good. Good anger "finds no joy in unrighteousness, but rejoices with the truth" (1 Corinthians 13:6). It sees evil as evil and refuses to change the rules to accommodate sin. This anger at injustice and wrongdoing is not to be allowed the room to fester into bitterness or rage. A writer for Desiring God Ministries, Jonathan Parnell, described this kind of anger in this way: "Anger is love in motion to deal with a threat to someone or something we truly care about."[28] This good anger deals with any threat to another's good like sin and idolatry. It is tempered and time-limited so that it does not open the door to the two threats of sin and Satan. Paul links the two when he continues, "And don't give the Devil an opportunity" (4:27). What is the connection between unchecked anger and the devil's activity?

An illustration of this relationship can be found in 2 Corinthians. Earlier Paul had sent a letter to the church at Corinth rebuking them for not dealing with open, shameful, yet unconfessed sin in her midst. The believers were saddened by their lack of obedience and repented, obeying Paul's command by rebuking the one caught in sin. In 2 Corinthians, Paul rejoices that his first letter was used by God's grace to stir a sense of indignation, zeal, and justice that led to repentance (2 Corinthians 7:11). Just as the Corinthian believers had repented, God graciously led the man they disciplined to repentance as well.

In addressing this circumstance, Paul shows the connection between anger left unchecked and Satan's scheming. In 2 Corinthians 2:6-11, Paul wrote the following:

> "The punishment inflicted by the majority is sufficient for that person. As a result, you should instead forgive and comfort him. Otherwise, this one may be overwhelmed by excessive grief. Therefore I urge you to reaffirm your love to him. I wrote for this purpose: to test your character to see if you are obedient in everything. If you forgive anyone, I do too. For what I have forgiven — if I have forgiven anything — it is for you in the presence of Christ. I have done this so that we may not be taken advantage of by Satan. For we are not ignorant of his schemes."

---

[28] Jonathan Parnell, "What Our Anger Is Telling Us," published at www.desiringgod. org/blog on May 22, 2014.

The church was moved by indignation and outrage (the good kind) to rebuke the one caught in sin among them. He repented by God's grace. Yet their anger lingered so that forgiveness and restoration wasn't quickly extended. Paul, aware of how vulnerable this situation was, wrote, "I have [forgiven him] so that we may not be taken advantage of by Satan." Even good anger, left to linger, is the playground of the evil one. Our anger, if it becomes a hindrance to forgiveness, drifts toward sin and Satan's activity. The Corinthians had put their guard down by letting the sun go down on their anger. Paul forgave the man caught in sin in order to show the Corinthians the safe way forward that protects them from Satan's scheming. Satan can use a good thing like indignation at sin to his advantage. The accuser exploits this unchecked, righteous anger by engendering feelings of excessive grief and condemnation. The community of grace becomes a community of judgment if anger is allowed to linger. Repentance should lead to restoration as quickly and as wisely as possible (Galatians 6:1).

We desire this. We need this. The fences of righteous anger protect us from the harmful effects of sin. In our heart of hearts, we all want an angry community. Without it, true love is exchanged for a mushy substitute.

A Giving Community

Ephesians 4:28 uncovers the governing principle at work in a community that unleashes the mystery with great potency into the world. Paul gives a vivid illustration of this new community-oriented ethic in the example of stealing: "The thief must no longer steal. Instead, he must do honest work with his own hands, so that he has something to share with anyone in need" (Ephesians 4:28). A thief takes from people. He covets and sees others as an obstacle to his pleasure, so he steals from them to get what he wants. But now, as a part of this new community that has been transformed by God's grace, he can no longer think that way. Why? Because this new community is not made up of takers but givers. (Notice that this new community is not made up of a bunch of righteous people but even thieves who have become followers of Christ!)

The governing principle at work among this new community is that other's interests are regarded as more important than their own selfish interests. People are not measured by the stuff they have nor are they seen as avenues to personal pleasure. God's grace turns thieves from blessing-stealers into blessing-givers. In Luke 19, Zacchaeus didn't merely return the stolen money. After meeting Jesus, he was willing to give back four times as much as he had stolen. The greedy turn generous when the gospel changes them. Work becomes an avenue, not to increase their "standard of living but their standard of giving."[29]

Think of how revolutionary this way of thinking is. Imagine a Monday morning when you feel unmotivated to go to work. What if the incentive to get up and get going was found in the thought, "I need to work so that I can meet my brother's need. I need to get paid so I can share." That's a radical approach to the everyday. Giving is the blessing that comes from working with your own hands. That kind of change is unlocked by the mystery. A radical other-centeredness is awakened. The mystery changes the Monday morning blues. The burden of greed has been displaced by the joy found in meeting other's needs.

Paul then moves from their hands to what they do with their mouths. The tongue is a small but powerful instrument. Our words have the ability to strengthen relationships or to tear them down. How does this new community-oriented ethic change the way we talk? Let's consider Ephesians 4:29: "No foul language is to come from your mouth, but only what is good for building up of someone in need, so that it gives grace to those who hear." When we replace unwholesome and unhelpful words with encouragement and grace, the needy are strengthened and our mouths testify to the presence of the mystery

---

[29] Randy Alcorn, *The Treasure Principle*, Multnomah Books, 2001, pg. 75.

at work among us. Giving begins permeating our approach to life. Who we will bless with our hands and who we can encourage with our mouths starts shaping our agenda for each day.

A Sticky Community

This community overcomes threats to its new identity. The traits that either chip away at unity or reinforce our unity form the context around Paul's next exhortations: "And don't grieve God's Holy Spirit. You were sealed by Him for the day of redemption" (Ephesians 4:30). This emphasis on the Spirit echoes something Paul said earlier in this chapter. At the beginning of chapter 4, Paul urged us to protect the unity of the Spirit in the bond of peace (Ephesians 4:3). Now, near the end of the same chapter, we are urged to not grieve the same Spirit of unity we have received. It is clear from the context that grieving the Holy Spirit involves harboring attitudes that threaten unity or doing harmful actions that betray unity. Consider how present the Spirit is among us in the church: these negative attitudes or actions inflict grief, not merely on our brothers and sisters in Christ, but on Him. He hears the words. He bears the grief. He feels the distance. The Spirit is saddened by disunity. Division disturbs Him.

In Ephesians 4:30, Paul echoes a passage in Isaiah where Israel, after the miraculous redemption from Egypt, grieved and rebelled against the very Presence that saved them. This story is used as the basis of this charge to the church. The church needs to heed the warning of Israel and not dishearten the very One whose presence secures her redemption. The church has a common hope in the day of redemption that should enable faithful, unity-preserving action in the present.

Love requires this hope. Without hope, love's motivation wanes. Love "bears all things, believes all things, hopes all things, endures all things" (1 Corinthians 13:7). In this verse, the bookends of bearing all things and enduring all things find their power in the middle: "believing all things" and "hoping all things." Endurance in love is fueled by a steadfast hope. This is why Paul anchors his charge to not grieve the Holy Spirit in the very future the Holy Spirit secures for us. After commanding us not to grieve the Spirit, Paul writes, "You were sealed by Him for the day of redemption" (Ephesians 4:30b). *We* are being kept by the Holy Spirit for the day of redemption.

There is always hope which means there are always resources to love. Even if we die a thousand little deaths to preserve our unity (even if they don't feel little at the time), the Spirit guarantees these sacrifices lead to life. Love is always possible when hope is always present. Our common destiny, secured by the Spirit, combats division. His presence makes us sticky. We stick it out. We stick together.

In Ephesians 4:31, Paul lists some attitudes that if tolerated, threaten the potency of the church's witness to the mystery. They unravel the threads that God is weaving together through us in the mystery. They undermine the unity at work through the gospel. Paul writes, "All bitterness, anger and wrath, shouting and slander must be removed from you, along with all malice" (4:31). Paul begins exposing the threats to unity by addressing "all bitterness" (Ephesians 4:31). We become masons, repairing the wall that Christ abolished when we let residual anger morph into bitterness. All of it must go, Paul declares. Every ounce of inner resentment that puts an invisible wall between us and our brother or sister must be gouged from our hearts. Anger and wrath must be uprooted and removed. Grace and encouragement must replace the shouting and slandering that so easily slip out. Careless critiques and negative generalizations ("every time . . ." or "you always . . .") that so quickly flow from our mouths in conflict must go. We no longer need to prove our point; we no longer need to defend ourselves.

If we get this vision for community, inflicting pain starts to hurt us more than it hurts them. We start sharing in the Holy Spirit's grief. A new kind of mortar enters our relationships – the kind that makes us stick together.

Paul concludes this verse with the tagline, "along with all malice." Malice is the evil thinking that desires to inflict pain on others. It is the part of us that used to dominate our thinking when we were our own protectors and preservers (Titus 3:3). When we looked after ourselves, our anger protected us from the attacks of others and our malice kept us on the attack, pushing people away if they got too close or hurt us too much. Anger was the shield and malice the bow that shot the hurtful arrows that pushed them back.

But God's mercy interrupted this vicious cycle of hurt. God became our protector and defender in the gospel so that we can put down our shields and lay down our bows. Mercy brings healing. God's kindness invades our hearts, giving us kind thoughts and kind intentions.

Paul mentions this kindness in the next verse, "And be kind and compassionate to one another, forgiving one another, just as God also forgave you in Christ" (Ephesians 4:32). God's actions toward us transform the way we do relationships. There is a "just as" element to our way of relating. It used to be "just as" they harmed us, we would harm them. But not now. A new way of belonging has begun: we treat others "just as" God has treated us.

Being re-created in God's likeness gives the corporate life of the church a new rhythm. God's actions reverberate through ours. Remember the story of how Julie repaired Bec's plate at the beginning of this book? I am sure it was a messy job. Super glue finds its way onto our fingers and under our fingernails and onto our tabletops. It has a stubbornness about it. The glue at work in the mystery to mend the world is no different. It creates a people who have a stickiness about them. It is not the stickiness or clinginess that has its roots in insecurity that's always looking for affirmation. It's not looking for love but looking for ways to love. This kind of stickiness has its roots in the mystery, the mystery where Christ has become our peace as He made "both groups one and tore down the dividing wall" (Ephesians 2:14). God's "sticky" plan to bring two together into one spills out and makes a sticky people. Our hearts have sticky ethics. Our relationships have a stubborn resiliency to them.

This resiliency is needed because this community is not perfect. Far from it. The thieves and liars who left their former lives for Jesus are still tempted to steal and lie. The thoughtless words still proceed from our mouths. The person who offended you will not be able to pay back how he hurt you or "reimburse" you for your time spent laboring to forgive him. That's okay. It hurts, yes. But God has treated us infinitely better than we deserve. And under the shadow of His grace, we too find the grace to forgive.

This mystery made unity is not superficial. It is real and tangible. These people do not give up on each other. They fight through adversity. The combination of grace, acceptance, and forgiveness forges their togetherness, unleashing God's mystery into the world with penetrating force.

In Turkey, we love to find new parks for our kids. City organizers have done a great job of dispersing different types of parks around our city. But most of the parks are crowded with lots of kids running everywhere. If they were not outside, the sheer volume of kids screaming would be too much to handle. Even in all the craziness, one thing never ceases to amaze me. When one of my sons trips and falls (because it's normally my boys that trip and fall), he immediately looks up to find me. In that one moment, if he can't find me, panic sets in. Others try to console him, but he wants none of it. Foreigners just won't do when he wants his father. Then I say his name. That's it. No yelling needed. My voice pierces through all the craziness and noise. His crying eyes catch mine. With outstretched arms and weeping relief, he cuts through the crowd and comes right to me.

All it takes is his father's voice. In a world of pushing and shoving and falling, the mystery finds a voice in churches that embrace the vision of

Ephesians 4. When this voice catches the ear of this broken world, something in it sounds so comforting, so right, so compelling. It not only pierces through the noise, but it resonates deep within. Hearing it alone brings a certain degree of peace. The world recognizes that voice. It doesn't sound foreign because it is the distinct voice of the One who created it.

The world is searching frantically for the voice that brings relief. May God find that voice through our unity.

CHAPTER 15

A New Rebellion

Ephesians 5:1-14

THE PROPHET JEREMIAH WARNED the people of Israel that they had settled for a peace that was no peace at all. False prophets had infiltrated Israel and encouraged people with a lie. They told them to settle down when their sin should have rendered them completely unsettled. Jeremiah remained true to God's message. He warned them that putting a stamp of peace on rebellion against God is perilous. The sword of God's wrath was coming while the people were being encouraged to take it easy. Some forms of peace are actually no peace at all. In essence, Jeremiah's prophetic ministry sought to disturb the peaceful so they might find true peace in repentance.

Paul's message to us through Ephesians echoes Jeremiah's. Our calling is to remain true to the Lord despite the disobedience that surrounds us. This type of rebellion actually promotes true peace. A community marked by continual repentance is actually safe though it may feel so vulnerable and weak. It refuses the false peace offered by the world's redefinition. It runs contrary or "rebels" against all false versions of unity. This may come as a surprise or might even sound contradictory, knowing what we know about the mystery thus far in Ephesians. Embodying the mystery in Chapter 5 ironically does not involve harmony but discord. It demands separation not integration. These two must remain two. Disunity, not unity, faithfully represents the mystery.

For the title of this chapter, I have labeled this corporate dissonance "rebellion." Rebellion is another way of saying nonconformity. It is a corporate lifestyle in Ephesians 5 that refuses to accept as normal what is abnormal.[30] It swims upstream, against the current of the culture that disregards God. Paul does not envision the church adopting a posture of antagonistic defiance in Ephesians 5. She shouldn't even seek to be odd for the sake of oddness. Her oddness stems from the reality that submission to Jesus is strange in this world turned upside down. We are called as "saints" and must maintain this holy peculiarity (Ephesians 5:3). We may seem irrelevant and out of touch. That's okay. It is in maintaining this distinction, however, that God's mystery is unleashed into the world.

"Worldliness," theologian David Wells writes, "is that system of values, in any given age, which has at its center our fallen human perspective, which displaces God and his truth from the world, and which makes sin look normal and righteousness seem strange."[31] The church cannot stamp peace on that which masquerades as the real thing. The mystery calls the church out of the world to an otherworldliness in the world. Her life offers an alternative, a counter-culture within the culture.

An Odd Purity

This new way of rebelling is God-ward in its orientation: "Therefore, be imitators of God, as dearly loved children" (Ephesians 5:1). God-likeness

---

[30] David Wells, *No Place for Truth*, Wm. B. Eerdmans Publishing Co., 1993, pg 215.

[31] David Wells, *Losing Our Virtue*, Wm. B. Eerdmans Publishing Co., 1998, pg. 4.

calibrates the church's moral compass. But this is not a burden; it is the expression of a loved child who loves to imitate his father. It's the plastic lawnmower that trails behind dad's real mower. It's the impulse of a loved child to be like the One who loves him so dearly. This conformity to God means nonconformity to the surrounding culture that is "excluded from the life of God" and "without God" in the world (Ephesians 4:18b, 2:12).

This God-ward orientation of the church should play out in how the church loves in a Godlike way. Christ's example of love forms the mold into which the church patterns its love. Thus Paul writes in Ephesians 5:2, "And walk in love, as the Messiah also loved us and gave Himself up for us, a sacrificial and fragrant offering to God." The church has been loved in such a way that transforms her ways of loving. How did He love? He loved out of utter regard for God. He offered Himself as "a sacrificial and fragrant offering to God" (Ephesians 5:2). We were not at the center of Christ's love for us. God was. He loved us for God, out of obedience to God, for the glory of God. This is what gave Christ's love its purity and distinctiveness.

Worldly ways of loving don't share this Godward orientation. Love is interpreted as love only if it serves the sovereign self of the person receiving love. Oprah Winfrey expresses this bent toward self-sovereignty under the guise of self-esteem when she writes, "Real self-esteem comes from being able to define the world in your own terms, by knowing where you stand and refusing to abide by the judgments of others. There will always be people trying to 'level' you or bring you down."[32] People who try to 'level' you are perceived threats to self-esteem and are thus deemed unloving. According to Oprah, the judgments of others are to be resisted because those judgments are unloving because they limit one's self-expression.

---

[32] Oprah Winfrey, "Oprah's Guide to Authentic Power," from http://www.oprahmag. co.za/live-your-best-life/self-development/oprah%E2%80%99s-guide-to-authentic-power. Posted October 2013.

The church inhabits a different world where Christ is king. She has been 'leveled' by a love so great that running her own life seems burdensome and unappealing. The illusion of freedom when self was king has been exchanged for the true freedom she has found in Christ's love. Christ's love defines her world. And it forms the framework through which she loves.

This God-ward orientation to Christ's love led to the purest expression of love ever witnessed. Christ's love wasn't tainted by narrow self-regard or tailored to our distorted way of receiving love. To please God, He loved us and gave Himself for us. He did not schedule a portion of His day or a segment of His life. He gave all. And the church, in like fashion, is to give her all so that God will be praised.

Pure Motives

Paul lists three actions in Ephesians 5:3 that diametrically oppose this sacrificial, self-giving love: "But sexual immorality and any impurity or greed should not even be heard of among you, as is proper for saints." Sexual immorality, impurity, and greed have nothing in common with the way Christ loved.

Sexual immorality has at its core two dynamics. First, it violates the God-ordained context of sexual expression: marriage. Pure love honors the sacredness of marriage because it values the God who created marriage. Second, sexual immorality uses others for personal pleasure. When we commit immorality, we reject God's way and invite others to join our rejection in order to give of themselves for our own pleasure. We put them on the altar of our pleasure and say, "Lay down your life." This invitation stands in stark contrast to the self-giving nature of Christ who took His place on the altar, offering Himself in our place. Sexual immorality actually opposes true love and has no place in the church. This narrowing of sexual pleasure to selfish desires is too boring for

God's people. Husbands and wives who out-serve one another in the bedroom embody the power of Christ's love and experience a new depth of satisfaction. Holiness does not confine us but releases us into further realms of happiness. The church's odd purity in her sexuality can be a powerful witness to a watching world.

Paul also mentions greed in Ephesians 5:3 because once again it diametrically opposes how Christ loved. Greedy people feed on people, and this mindset wrecks relationships. Hungry yet never satisfied, greed will not merely harm one relationship but many. Greed cannot be tolerated at any level among the church. It "should not even be heard of among you," Paul writes to the Ephesians (5:3b).

Paul reinforces the sober weight of his exhortation in verse 5 of this chapter when he writes, "For know and recognize this: every sexually immoral or impure or greedy person, who is an idolater, does not have an inheritance in the kingdom of the Messiah and of God." These behaviors reveal that a person's heart is out of tune with Christ's. These sins expose the idols at work in the human heart. This group, Paul warns, has no inheritance in the kingdom of Christ and God because an idol has taken Christ's rightful place. Those functional saviors will never deliver. Self-absorbed desires dictate their relationships. They have no share in Christ because they are not Christ's. The church must "know and recognize" the perils of unloving, idolatrous immorality (5:5). A God-ward purity should mark our motives.

Pure Speech

The way the church speaks becomes another avenue to display the distinctiveness of God's people in Ephesians 5:3: "Coarse and foolish talking or crude joking are not suitable, but rather giving thanks." Why is giving of thanks contrasted with coarse, foolish talking and crude joking? Crude joking has an air about it of entitlement and arrogance.

The man who talks big feels big. Being rude stems from feeling big in a small world of rights. Rude ways of speaking are rooted in entitled ways of thinking. Saying "thank you," on the other hand, stems from humility. Thankful people feel small in a big world of undeserved blessings. They don't feel entitled to anything because grace permeates their perspective. Every blessing points their mind back to the abundant grace they found in Christ Jesus. They join Paul's litany of praises in Ephesians 1 because every earthly blessing reminds them of God's blessings found in Christ.

Foolish talk ignores God as the Giver of every good gift: "A fool says in his heart, 'God does not exist'" (Psalm 14:1). Cynical people inhabit a self-conceived world where God is not needed or entirely absent. And they talk to themselves and to the world accordingly. On the other hand, thankful people feel unworthy. A people saved by grace talk like it. We must ask ourselves: what is coming out of our mouths? If the world listened in, would they find a thankful people?

People who have an "inheritance in the kingdom of the Messiah and of God" live other-worldly lives (Ephesians 5:5b). Our joyful resistance testifies of the joy to be had when His kingdom comes. A new rebellion has begun. A new people have been born.

The writer Richard Lovelace once said, "In the hearts of the people is a groping, inarticulate conviction that, if the right ruler would only come along, the world would be healed of all its wounds. Creation is headless and desperately searching for its head."[33] A distinct church like Ephesians 5 envisions reveals to the world that the search is over. The right Ruler has come.

---

[33] Richard Lovelace, *Renewal as a Way of Life: A Guidebook for the Spiritual Life,* Wipf and Stock Publishers, 2002. pg. 41.

CHAPTER 16

An Odd Intolerance

Ephesians 5:6-14

"Let no one deceive you with empty arguments, for God's wrath is coming on the disobedient because of these things. Therefore, do not become their partners. For you were once darkness, but now you are light in the Lord. Walk as children of light — for the fruit of the light results in all goodness, righteousness, and truth — discerning what is pleasing to the Lord. Don't participate in the fruitless works of darkness, but instead expose them. For it is shameful even to mention what is done by them in secret. Everything exposed by the light is made clear, for what makes everything clear is light. Therefore it is said: Get up, sleeper, and rise up from the dead, and the Messiah will shine on you" (Ephesians 5:6-14).

THE CHURCH MUST PRESERVE her rebellious streak. Flirting with the world's ways would be to deny her calling. We must maintain our distinctiveness, Paul writes, "Therefore, do not become their partners."

The mystery now revealed presses the universe toward unity in Christ. One would think discord and division would deny the mystery. "Just erase the differences, accept one another, and we will become one," the world might say. But not so fast. The unifying dynamic at work through the mystery has a distinct quality to it. It is not void of truth. It has nothing to do with the modern view of tolerance that means universal acceptance. When the world equates tolerance with unquestioning support of my moral choices, we have a problem. This is the world's version of its own mystery. In this parasitic version, the world keeps the two as two but encourages them to hug. True unity is not warm feelings between two individuals. The mystery goes deeper. It overcomes the obstacles that keep the two as two and brings the two into one in Christ. We cannot be one if our individuality is the highest value. Christ creates oneness in our diversity. The world waves the white flag of peace while true peace with God and with one another eludes its grasp. Erasing the distinctions between truth and error actually closes the door to unity. True unity is exchanged for a counterfeit substitute. Universal acceptance actually undermines the true acceptance at work in the mystery.

Keeping in step with God's program in the mystery and out of step with the world's false version requires discerning ears and diligent feet. "Let no one deceive you . . ." and "Pay careful attention, then, to how you walk," Paul writes in Chapter 5. Everything anti-mystery and anti-gospel (read: anti-unity) must be opposed. If the church is to walk worthy, she must keep her edge. God certainly hasn't lost His: "for God's wrath is coming on the disobedient because of these things" (Ephesians 5:6b).

At first glance, God's anger seems to be at odds with His plan to end hostility through the mystery. How can God's anger and God's peace-making endeavors coexist?

God's wrath currently shapes the experiences of the "disobedient" in verse 6b. A more literal translation would be the "sons of disobedience." These terms describe the unbelieving world. They have a habitual, defiant posture toward God. Thus Paul labels them "sons of disobedience," and not merely those who disobey. They are walking "according to the course of this world" and the "children under wrath" according to Ephesians 2:2-3. They know nothing of repentance.

God's wrath currently presses in on them because of their deeds. God, in His righteous wrath, grants sinners the fulfillment of the very desires that end up betraying them. Sin carries its own judgment and penalty by God's just decree. Sin self-destructs. Debauchery spirals downward. Sexual immorality, greed, and impurity, the three aspects of disobedience Paul mentions in Chapter 5, stem from idolatry. The human heart is a manufacturing plant that pumps out idol after idol, sin after sin.

God's wrath functions in two ways in the world. Sometimes He reveals the brokenness of idolatry by opening the world's eyes to its hopelessness. At other times, His wrath hides the brokenness for a season. Sometimes the idols seem sufficient and at other times insufficient. The feeling of unsatisfaction *and satisfaction* can both be God's wrath against all idolatry. Some experience a temporary heaven on earth while others endure hell from their idol of choice. Some gain the world; others lose the world. But both lose their souls. They live under God's wrath, just in different ways.

This is why it is important for the church to discern everything she hears. God's wrath does not send a lightning bolt from heaven every time the disobedient disobey. It works in ways hidden from the natural eye. His wrath may be revealed in letting sinners go their own way in luxury or self-destruction. We cannot equate prosperity with God's blessing or poverty with God's curse. In this modern-day Gotham where sometimes the bad guys win and the good guys lose, Paul's exhortation to the church makes sense: "Let no one deceive you with empty arguments, for God's wrath is coming on the disobedient because of these things" (Ephesians 5:6).

The world casts off restraint in this time when God delays judgment. The world assumes it is free from accountability. That is a dangerous assumption. The feeling itself evidences God's wrath upon them. God is not mocked. "No! You will not die!" the serpent told Eve (Genesis 3:4). No way, serpent! Evil will be judged so. Idolatry never goes unnoticed in heaven. The church must remain soberly attentive to God's word and to her wayward heart to remain faithful.

Discernment is needed because she faces the danger of worldliness. Worldliness creeps around unnoticed. Those who know they are sick go to the doctor. But worldliness can make you feel healthier in this upside-down world.[34] Disobedience may give a "peace" because it cloaks its soul-destroying dynamic in the currents of popular opinion. Satan crept into the church at Corinth through false teachers as an angel of light (2 Corinthians 11:14-15). These teachers expound "empty arguments" in Ephesians 5. This doctrine simply does not accord with Christ - they may talk about Him but in the end deny Him. They may be bestsellers on the Christian book list but have nothing in common with Christ. They may quote the Bible but actually undervalue submission to the Bible. The church must be on guard. God refuses to tolerate any teaching that pulls people away from Christ. A tolerance for error is a troubling sign for any church.

The church must share God's intolerance: "Therefore, do not become their partners" (Ephesians 5:7). Becoming their partner would mean betraying our identity as "saints" (Ephesians 5:3b). The church's moral compass must stay calibrated to the Word and not the world. Our feet must stick to God's path. Thus Paul reminds us "For you were once darkness," in Ephesians 5:8, "But now you are light in the Lord." A categorical shift has happened. The Lord has transferred us to the light, so now we are to "walk as children of

---

[34] From a video featuring David Wells in preparation for the 2006 Desiring God National Conference on www.desiringgod.org.

light - for the fruit of the light results in all goodness, righteousness, and truth - discerning what is pleasing to the Lord" (8b-10).

But walking in the light does not translate into a life of moral perfection. Listen to John's description of "walking in the light" in 1 John 1:7-9:

> "But if we walk in the light as He Himself is in the light, we have fellowship with one another, and the blood of Jesus His Son cleanses us from all sin. If we say, 'We have no sin,' we are deceiving ourselves, and the truth is not in us. If we confess our sins, He is faithful and righteous to forgive us our sins and to cleanse us from all unrighteousness."

What separates light from darkness according to John? Not the presence of sin but the presence of unconfessed sin. The light produces repentant confession, which purifies the church as the blood of Christ cleanses her of all unrighteousness. A community of light is not arrogant about its brightness. It is just the opposite. It shines because it refuses to blame someone or something else for its sins. It owns its own darkness and wants something better. It refuses to tolerate its own sin so it keeps clinging to the blood of Christ as its only hope. This community lets Christ's blood have the last word. It lets Him raise the white flag. Refusing to tolerate its own evil makes this community oddly intolerant.

The Fruit of Light

In Ephesians 5:9 and following, Paul shows what kind of community this intolerance creates. He begins, "For the fruit of the light results in all goodness, righteousness, and truth" (5:9). Repentance, in its habitual posture of godly sorrow at sin and God-ward forsaking of sin, characterizes this new community of rebels. This open acknowledgement and disowning of sin keeps the healing light of God's presence and grace shining. "Hiding" sin simply conforms to the world and invites more darkness. "The difference between a Christian and a non-Christian," Pastor Mark Dever teaches, "is when a non-Christian is convicted of sin, he sides with his sin. When a Christian is convicted of sin, he sides with God, against himself."[35] This posture of being "against himself" with Christ ironically opens the possibility of a person being "for the community." This intolerance for personal sin generates the wholesome fruit that Paul describes in Ephesians 5.

Darkness fortifies itself through defensiveness. The church has every reason to be less defensive and more self-suspicious. She knows her former rebellion ran deep. She can stand against herself because Someone else stands on her behalf. Jesus advocates for her before the Father - what other defense need she muster? The criticism and condemnation she deserved fell upon Him. Prying eyes are welcome among the community that walks in the Light. The worst exposure of her sin has already happened at the cross.

> "Who can bring an accusation against God's elect? God is the One who justifies. Who is the one who condemns? Christ Jesus is the One who died, but even more, has been raised; He also is at the right hand of God and intercedes for us" (Romans 8:33-34).

Before we move from here, a subtle misapplication of these truths has crept into some churches. These churches boast of being a hospital for sinners where sick sinners are welcome. This is gloriously true, but just realizing our own sickness and coming in to receive treatment is not the goal. Good hospitals go further. They work to restore the sick. Patients themselves aren't okay with remaining sick or they would have stayed home. The whole point of calling the doctor is to get better. The church is indeed a hospital for the sick, but we cannot stop there.

---

[35] From a sermon Mark Dever delivered during the 2009 Bethlehem Pastor's Conference in Minneapolis, Minnesota.

This half-application of a great truth creates a culture that unintentionally celebrates failure by encouraging openness without moving to repentance. They follow "We are not okay" with "and that's okay." We are not okay, true. "That's okay" is true as well because only because God sent a Redeemer. But we have to move from "and that's okay" to "we're also not okay with not being okay." This important step from receiving the diagnosis to initiating the treatment initiates the process of getting better. We must move from mere confession of sin to grace-empowered crucifying of our sin. Now, we might move from one doctor to another or from one treatment to another, but at least we are healthier than when we came in.

Notice the result of this lifestyle infused with God's light: "all goodness, righteousness, and truth" (Ephesians 5:8). These are contrasted with the "fruitless works of darkness" in verse 11. Walking in God's pure light produces relational health and wholeness: goodness, righteousness, and truth. Running from God enslaves but running to God produces real freedom and real depth in relationships. In the relational wreckage of our age, who wouldn't welcome tasting goodness, righteousness, and truth?

We don't have to go far to see the fruit of darkness in our world. Sexual immorality, which Paul mentioned earlier in this chapter, actually hollows out human relationships, even though at the same time it engenders a sense of connection. The sexually immoral become slaves of one another, chained to the selfish desires of their partner. They cannot break free because that would be forsaking the one who promises them the fulfillment of their own selfish desires. This is why dating relationships that are sexually immoral find it hard to break up or break free. They are trapped as a slave to their slave.

I recently talked with a man whose wife cheated on him with another man. The tearful hurt in his eyes captured the anguish of betrayal. That pain is the fruit of darkness. The bitterness of adultery was written all over his face. His marriage did not start that way. No one envisions that sadness on the big day. Tearful feelings of shame and betrayal had replaced the tearful joy that accompanied his wedding day.

His face brought me back to another face I used to see regularly. As I mentioned earlier, I used to officiate a lot of weddings. The faces of these new couples radiated that joy of relational bliss. These couples honored the sacredness of marriage by refusing to flirt with darkness. They didn't cross the line sexually until they were in the safe, free confines of marriage. Some even refused to kiss until they heard me say, "You may kiss the bride." They had waited and waited for that moment and the joy of their prolonged purity gushed over onto all of us who gathered to witness their wedding. We tasted the fruit of light: "goodness, righteousness, and truth." That was joy in its rarest, purest form. Everyone who gathered knew that the couple hadn't missed out on anything. They had gained everything. Honoring God's boundaries for human sexuality leads to pure, honest, beautiful relationships.

The church is to be an agent of that rarified joy in the world. The honesty and integrity with which we conduct our relationships serves as a refuge in the midst of the relational turmoil surrounding us. Unrighteous relationships resound with insecurity: "Where is he?" "What is she doing?" "What is he seeing on the Internet?" Unrighteousness unsettles, but righteousness breeds trust. It enables relational rest. The world should be able to peer into the church, not to her perfection, but to her discontentment with her imperfections and her stubborness about progress. The world should see relationships that deal honestly with sin while holding on to each other in love. They refuse to let sin sever the bond that Christ has created. They are hostile against sin, not against each other. Grace enables us to be who we are as we are but not stay where we are. The mystery allows us to see beyond our own darkness to the light of the God who is picking up the broken pieces.

The sweet fruit of righteousness, truth, and goodness has another result that is captured in Ephesians 5:10: "discerning what is pleasing to the Lord."

Righteousness leads to more righteousness. Our moral compass is shaped by our moral choices. The same goes for darkness: immorality leads to more immorality. Disobedience shrivels the ability to discern. Obedience expands it.

If you want to know God's will, start doing the things you know He has commanded. Walk in the light. Get as close to Him as possible. Love your brothers and sisters. And just wait: the world of what pleases Him will open before you. Finding what pleases Him stems from following what pleases Him. The fruit of light comes as it opens the path to more light.

The Function of Light

The fruit of light is tasted by every church that welcomes it. It exposes and purges darkness on the inside. Paul now moves from the fruit of light in 5:9-10 to discuss the function of the light for those on the outside. It has a broader function. The light shines into the world through the community, giving the darkness an opportunity to see its own darkness and come to the light. This light comes infused with hope-enabling potential. Paul moves the discussion to this effect of light in Ephesians 5:11-14:

> "Don't participate in the fruitless works of darkness, but instead expose them. For it is shameful even to mention what is done by them in secret. Everything exposed by the light is made clear, for what makes everything clear is light. Therefore it is said: Get up, sleeper, and rise up from the dead, and the Messiah will shine on you."

This new rebel community must be more than nonconformist. They could become monastic and just exist alongside the fallen world. But that would not unleash the mystery. It's not just steering clear of the world's values and vices. Avoidance is not full faithfulness. The church's responsibility reaches further, "Don't participate in the fruitless works of darkness, but instead expose them" (Ephesians 5:11). Active resistance and enlightening engagement are required if others are to see the light of what God is up to in the mystery.

The reason why Paul commands the church to expose darkness is twofold - one is positive and the other negative. The negative reason Paul mentions first. It is the shameless shame of the world's deceptive and secretive ways that presses the church to act: "For it is shameful even to mention what is done by them in secret" (Ephesians 5:12). These secret deeds must be exposed for their true colors. Simple coexistence could be interpreted as approval. But the evils are too evil to let go unchecked. The light must bring them out into the open. The church, by her distinct character, is to be a voice of reason in a culture gone awry. Where the world's conscience has gone silent, the church must keep her voice. The church must blush when the world has forgotten how to. Like the sunrise to a captain lost at sea, this light may guide the world to realize just how far off course it has drifted.

The next part of verse 13 and the beginning of verse 14 captures Paul's positive motivation for the church to expose the darkness: "Everything exposed by the light is made clear, for what makes everything clear is light." In this verse, the light becomes a beacon through which the church illumines the world, not a realm of life in which the church lives (like verses 8-9). The world receives some degree of grace through the presence of the church. Her righteous anger that calls sin "sin" preserves the world from its own perilous moral judgment. The church sounds the alarm when the world sleepwalks near the cliff's edge. This light that illumines the darkness resonates through the peaceful sit-ins of Rosa Parks. This light shines through Christians who adopt unwanted babies who are about to be aborted in secret clinics of urban centers across the globe. The church, in her distinct character and her nonconforming dissonance, affords the world an opportunity to look at life through a different lens. Light is a gift to the darkness even if the darkness doesn't appreciate it.

Paul continues to show the function of light in verse 14: "Therefore it is said, Get up, sleeper, and rise up from the dead, and the Messiah will shine on you." This is a quote from a hymn that was known by both Paul and the believers at Ephesus. This hymn captures images from the book of Isaiah. These truths remind believers of how we came into the light. We were sleepwalking through life, dead in our sins, conforming to the world's system when resurrection light dawned on us. This quotation would have the modern-day effect in most churches of reading these words from Charles Wesley: "Long my imprisoned spirit lay, fast bound in sin and nature's night; Thine eye diffused a quickening ray - I woke the dungeon flamed with light; My chains fell off, my heart was free, I rose, went forth, and followed Thee."[36] Both of these hymns recall the process by which Jesus' resurrecting light illumined the dark dungeon of our death and brought us to life. The light functions to impart life.

Why is this reminder needed? Resignation is a possible response to the evil that surrounds us. We might accept the way things are as unchangeable. We will not shine the light if we believe the darkness will not or cannot change. "What's the point?" we might wonder. Paul's hymn keeps us from acquiescing to the status quo. This hymn stirs a resilient hope that refuses to yield to pervasive darkness. Why? Because the sovereign, death-overcoming power of God's light is still shining.

Light pushes back darkness. That's our story. Other stories have yet to be told: "Everything exposed by the light is made clear" (Ephesians 5:13).

A few years ago, a pastor from Idaho, Doug Wilson, and an atheist speaker and writer, Christopher Hitchens, engaged in a debate published in *Christianity Today* entitled "Is Christianity Good for the World?" Hitchens was an antagonistic atheist, seeking to expose Wilson's errors and narrow thinking. Sometimes he did it kindly, sometimes rudely. The dialogue went back and

---

[36] Charles Wesley, "And Can It Be?" *Psalms and Hymns*, 1738.

forth from blog post to blog post. When the debate finally came to a close, Wilson concluded with this compelling invitation to come to Christ:

> "He [God] has established his great but welcoming household, and there is room enough for you. Nothing you have ever said or done will be held against you. Everything will be washed and forgiven. There is simple food — bread and wine — on the table. The door is open, and we'll leave the light on for you."[37]

The church that believes the mystery keeps the door open and the light on for the world in darkness. Keeping the light on for those in darkness sounds a lot like winsome faithfulness to Ephesians Chapter 5.

---

[37] Doug Wilson, Blog Post "Is Christianity Good for the World?" on Christianity Today, June 1, 2007.

CHAPTER 17

A Strange Sobriety

Ephesians 5:15-21

LTHOUGH I LIVE IN Central Asia, I was in the States recently and
met a Turkish man who owned his own cell phone repair shop at a
local mall. Sitting with him and watching him work was fascinating.
Worried customers with cracked screens and water damaged phones came
in every day. He opened their phones and screw-by-screw (each tiny screw
is different!), and piece-by-piece he assessed the damage. He replaced the
broken parts and pieced the phone back together. If he wasn't careful in
how he disassembled the phone, reassembly became frustratingly difficult.
If the tiny screws get scattered everywhere, a 20-minute job could last an
hour. He has to honor the design of the company that created the phone
or there is no hope for it ever working again. One screw misplaced or lost
could mean trouble.

This picture of attentiveness to detail and submission to the designer
reminded me of Ephesians 5:15-6:9. As the church experiences God's grace
in her own brokenness, she is reassembled. Ephesians 5 reveals two facets
of this healing process that are critical for the church to embrace: sobriety
and submission. Sobriety is the church's earnest attentiveness to the details

of God's wisdom. Submission, which we will discuss in the next chapter, is her acceptance of the way He ordered the world. The world wants neither. It walks in ignorance to God's wisdom and fails to see the goodness in the order of its Designer. Then it wonders why it can't be fixed.

The church's sobriety and submissiveness seem strange in any culture, for it represents a new way of being repaired. Both of these marks distinguish the church from the world which marches along its path of defiance. This new way is by God's grace, and this grace brings a whole new order to how we approach all of life, which is outlined in Ephesians 5:15-6:9. We will focus on 5:15-21 in this chapter and save the rest of this section for the next chapter.

In the last chapter we reflected on Ephesians 5:6-14 and studied how Paul charged the church to have discernment and to live distinctly. Verses 15-18's contribution to that discussion reveals the church's need for intentionality and diligence. It shows how the mystery changes our relationship to time. The term sobriety captures this earnest attentiveness to God's wisdom well. It's a level-headed seriousness to all of life. In Ephesians 5:15-18, Paul commands us to embody this sobriety, to have a weightiness that recognizes the significance of time:

> "Pay careful attention, then, to how you walk - not as unwise people but as wise - making the most of the time, because the days are evil. So don't be foolish, but understand what the Lord's will is. And don't get drunk with wine, which leads to reckless actions, but be filled with the Spirit" (Ephesians 5:15-18).

Churches don't gravitate toward wisdom. It must be sought: "Furthermore, if you call out to insight and lift your voice to understanding, if you seek it like silver and search for it like hidden treasure, then you will understand the fear of the LORD and discover the knowledge of God" (Proverbs 2:3-5).

Paul had already pursued this wisdom on behalf of the Ephesian believers. In Chapter 1, he prayed, "I pray that the God of our Lord Jesus Christ, the glorious Father, would give you a spirit of wisdom and revelation in the knowledge of Him" (Ephesians 1:17). Time will be treasured when God is treasured. The wise sobriety of Ephesians 5 is the result of seeing God. Chapter 1's prayer empowers obedience to the appeal of chapter 5.

Paul gives a positive motivation with a negative reinforcement for his exhortation in verse 16. Positively, we should seize each moment that we have been entrusted by "making the most of the time" (5:16a). This is not referring to time as in the 24-hour time period of every day but to the God-appointed moments that come infused with meaning and purpose. Paul's point is for us to capitalize on every God-ordained opportunity. Slumbering in drunken recklessness, which Paul will address in verse 18, ignores the seriousness of the moment. Laziness breeds folly. Alertness to recognize and capitalize on that intersection where God's mission and our routine cross – that's "making the most of the time." The God-infused possibilities that make every moment significant motivate the church to diligence.

The potential for good in the everyday routines of life inspires us to be ready for action. But the potential for evil also exists. The negative reinforcement of why we need to apply ourselves to wisdom is "because the days are evil" (5:16b). Time, in one sense, is not on God's side or our side as the church. God administrates the mystery against the grains of sand. His redemptive plan presses human history toward unity in Christ while history, if left to itself, drifts toward chaos and fragmentation. Time is not neutral. It is anti-God, anti-mystery. There is no inherent redemptive quality in time.

Paul continues, "So don't be foolish, but understand what the will of the Lord is" (5:17). Ephesians 1 equates the "will of God" with the mystery where God is at work reconciling all things in Jesus. "Wisdom" keeps in step with this plan to end division in Jesus. A church cultivates this wisdom when its members approach each day alertly, aligning their relationships, prayers, and priorities with God's program for the world. It would be folly to stay behind a veil when God has removed it and revealed His plan for the world.

It's folly to do anything that desensitizes our discernment to walk in accordance with God's program in the mystery (Ephesians 5:18a). Drunkenness must be avoided. Recklessness does not lead to restoration or repair. This sober sensitivity needs the Spirit of God. Being filled with His fullness keeps us in tune with God's wisdom and in step with God's ways. That is why "being filled with the Spirit" in 5:18 is contrasted with "getting drunk with wine."

Being filled with the Spirit results in a distinct community that speaks differently to one another:

> "Speaking to one another in psalms, hymns, and spiritual songs, singing and making music from your heart to the Lord, giving thanks always for everything to God the Father in the name of our Lord Jesus Christ, submitting to one another in the fear of Christ" (Ephesians 5:19-21).

The Spirit produces a God-ward orientation to all of life. The church persistently praises God, giving thanks in the name of the Lord Jesus Christ (5:19a, 5:20b). Each individual sings and makes music to the Lord from his or her heart. The Spirit's filling results in a distinct manner of relating to one another. Individuals begin submitting to one another out of reverence for Christ's supremacy which transforms how they approach marriage, work, and family (5:21-6:9). They speak truth and words of hope to one another via psalms and spiritual songs. Paul just quoted one of these hymns in verse 14 that reminded us of Christ's life-giving power. This kind of gospel-centered encouragement reverberates through the community that is filled with the Holy Spirit. Humility, hope, and thanksgiving mark the community where the Spirit's fullness is present.

Church life according to Ephesians 5:15-21 has a sobriety about it. We do not waste time together. We only have so much of it, so we are precise and deliberate in our use of it. We develop a culture of discernment where the hard questions are asked. We consciously turn our corporate conversations into rehearsals of God's grace. Giving thanks to God and honoring one another becomes the rhythm to our corporate life. We look different because we are different. The fullness of God's Spirit heightens our sensitivities to God's activity and grace, flooding our corporate life with songs of His praise.

This corporate intentionality stands out in a world that cannot wait for the weekend. With our conversations, our meditations, and our management of time, there is a deliberateness that marks our time together. We have an odd sobriety about us. Today, even in the mundane, we could have front row seats to behold more of the mystery unfolding before our very eyes.

One afternoon, as I watched my friend repair an iPhone, another couple came in with an iPad that had stopped working. The wireless was broken, and they had never backed it up to the cloud or a computer. My friend opened it to assess what went wrong. The couple had attempted to fix what they could, but the issue proved too complex and their meddling may have made it worse. My friend made a few adjustments and plugged it into his computer to restore it, but it would not restore. It wouldn't even reboot. The woman's face froze. She stared at my friend as the news sunk in. Baby pictures, memories, contacts – everything was lost. There was no backup. She looked at her husband. They walked out dejected in the sad realization that there was nothing they could do and that they should have come in earlier.

May our sobriety help people come in before it's too late. The hope for restoration remains.

CHAPTER 18

Christ Is No Lord Business

Ephesians 5:21-6:9

ONE OF MY FAVORITE movies to watch with my kids is *The Lego Movie*. In the movie there is a tyrant named "Lord Business" who wants to eliminate creativity and freedom by controlling the Lego world by force. His instrument to accomplish this is the "kragle." The Lego world, however, does not realize he is a tyrant. He has successfully spun a media campaign that has left them thinking everything is awesome. Lord Business's agenda is basically a worldly attempt at unity through conformity and forced submission. In Ephesians language, it's his own version of the "mystery." Suppression and deceit is one way to force the two pieces to become one.

The whole movie becomes a commentary on authority and unity. What vision will "Lord" the world? One vision of authority enforces control by putting everything on lockdown. The kragle represents this oppressive way to establish order through constrained conformity. Some people refuse to buy it. They are the resistance movement and they hold fast to a different vision for the world. They are led by a group called the "master builders." Their creativity allows them to use Legos to create new machines that resist the confines of Lord Business's controlled order. They want to be free so that they can use their creativity to express their diversity. They want to use the Legos - not glue the Legos.

Whose vision for the future wins? Controlled order or creative freedom? What if this is a false dichotomy? Are these two things at odds? The mystery in Ephesians says "no." Just what kind of "Lord" is Christ? Is He just another suppressive ruler whose goal is to force conformity in order to create unity? What is His kingdom going to be like? Ephesians reveals He is no Lord Business and God's version of the mystery needs no kragle. God's program through Christ is piecing a world together where two want to fit together as one - where order and freedom coexist in Christ. God envisions a world of peaceful order and a world of creative freedom – that is His agenda in the mystery. We will never be more ourselves than we will be in that world and we will never be more unified. That's the world God is preparing for us in the days of fulfillment when His kingdom comes and He brings everything together in the Messiah (Ephesians 1:10).

The problem is that the world sees Christ as "Lord Business." They perceive Him as a cosmic killjoy who enforces His laws in order to put the place on lockdown. They mistakenly sense the kragle on His hands and form a resistance movement so that they can save their individuality and creativity. His authority, in their view, suppresses and limits them and as a result, they want independence and freedom.

But they miss the true beauty of the mystery. God's vision for the world through Christ brings perfect freedom and perfect order. The mystery is mending a world where submission and satisfaction are not at odds with one another. It is a world of forever-flourishing under the dominion of a Forever King.

The church is the present embodiment of that kingdom on earth. She has stopped resisting because she sees the beauty of His plan. She submits to

Christ as Head over all. The truth has opened her eyes to see just how awesome everything will be when His kingdom comes. The Spirit orients the church to see goodness and freedom in God's ordering of the world. This submissive spirit plays out in three everyday contexts in Ephesians 5:22-6:9: marriage, family, and work.

Submission to Christ and to one another in these contexts results from being filled with the Spirit. Paul explains this result in Verse 21: "submitting to one another in the fear of Christ." The Spirit-filled community reveres Christ as Lord and respects earthly forms of authority.

With each picture of submission, Paul never lets Christ leave the focus. There is a Christ-wardness to this submission; it occurs "in the fear of Christ" (5:21). For example, this supreme regard for Christ is found in the charge to wives: "Wives submit to your own husbands as to the Lord . . . Now as the church submits to Christ, so wives are to submit to their husbands in everything" (5:22, 24). This ultimate regard for Christ is also found in the charge to children: "Children, obey your parents as you would the Lord," (6:1a). It echoes through the charge to slaves in 6:5: "Slaves, obey your human masters with fear and trembling, in the sincerity of your heart, as to Christ" (6:5).

This is what gives Christian submissiveness its oddness in this world. We live on a different plane. We inhabit a different universe where authority structures are valued as expressions of Christ's lordship. Our joyful submission to His design echo the joys that will be when His kingdom comes and His will is done on earth as it is in heaven. Being recreated means that the new world has begun shaping our life as the church. Our eyes have been reopened to the goodness of His structured world. We come into the community of grace to be freed from this world's broken system.

Our submissiveness does not stem from the relative worthiness or unworthiness of the person in authority over us. It is the Lord Christ we serve.

The Spirit empowers us to submit by seeing beyond the earthly authorities to the One who stands above all: the Lord Christ. The Spirit's fullness results in full submission, in every way and every context, to Christ as Lord.

This submissiveness becomes a potent picture of the mystery. The unity of harmonious homes and workplaces gives shape to the world's vision of God's gracious agenda. The goodness of how God brings order to our chaos becomes visible in submissive marriages, families, and work relationships. God Himself has stepped into our brokenness, assessed the damage, and now has begun repairing. And He is good at it.

Submission in Marriage

Submissive wives demonstrate the power of the gospel. Paul bookends the section on marriage with the wife's responsibility because submissiveness is the main idea he wants to develop: "Wives, submit to your own husbands as to the Lord" (5:22) and "To sum up, each one of you is to love his wife as himself, and the wife is to respect her husband" (5:33). Wives demonstrate this nonconformity to the world through Spirit-empowered submission to their husbands. They embrace the Designer's plan.

Part of the judgment upon women after sin entered the world included the struggle to be content in her role in marriage. This judgment is why submission does not come naturally or easily to women. Her fallen nature wants to usurp God's established order for the family. She craves the headship Adam relegated when he put her in danger. That tragic story and God's judgment upon the woman is found in Genesis 3 where God tells Eve, "Your desire will be for your husband, yet he will rule over you" (Genesis 3:16b). This desire creates tension in her heart when she is called to rest her life in her husband's hands. She desires to turn the order in marriage on its head because she has this impulse to lead. Eve's story echoes through the countless stories of wives who inwardly distrust their husbands and are embittered against their leadership. But submissive wives tell a different story.

Spirit-filled wives highlight the goodness of God's design in marriage through joyful submission to Christ and to their husbands. "Submission" feels oppressive, enslaving, or denigrating to the modern mind, but the picture in Ephesians 5 has nothing in common with those words. Every Christian wife has a sacred privilege before her. She can, by her submissive spirit, show the world what it means to *be dependent on* and *to defer to* a loving leader whose love compels her utmost respect.

Wives and husbands are equal before God. There is no qualitative attachment to the idea of submission. Her worth is defined by her status as God's image-bearer and not her role as her husband's helper. They are equal in worth, but different in role (Genesis 1:27, 2:18). That is the beauty of this picture of marital "protocol." Calling on the wife to submit in the Bible does not make her second-class. It just puts her second in the order of marriage.

Or does it? What if the one who has the primary responsibility to lead puts her interests first? What's the order now?

The husband has a Christ-ward responsibility as well in this passage. And it's a game-changer. "Husbands," Paul exhorts, "love your wives, just as Christ loved the church and gave Himself for her" (5:25). Paul spends the bulk of his time in Ephesians 5:22-33 unpacking how Christ sacrificially loves the church, even going as far as dying in her place. Husbands are to take their cues from Christ who "gives Himself," "cares," and "provides" for his own body, the church (5:25-29). Husbands, by their selfless regard for the good of their wives, paint a picture for the world to behold the wondrous love of Christ. Christ's love creates a secure environment in which the church lives freely. A husband's love for his wife should compel this freedom. In this loving environment, submission becomes liberating. It rescues the wife from the oppressive burden of having to prove herself or provide for herself.

He is for her as she is. He is mindful of her wherever she is. He has her best interests at heart. She rests in beautiful deference to the love of another just as the church rests in Christ's love.

The wife plays the part of the church in this "drama" of marriage. This restful reliance on her husband's leadership magnifies the privilege of the church to have her future secured by Christ. Believing wives magnify the glory of Christ's love by Spirit-filled submission to their husbands. The world gets a taste, in living color, of what joyful deference to the able hands of Another looks like in action. For the church, independence from Him would be unthinkable. That kind of freedom has lost its appeal for wives whose husbands operate in the shadow of Christ's love for the church. She is far better with Him than apart from Him. The church simply cannot find a better love than she has found in Jesus. Submission becomes the reflex of a heart so loved.

If I notice my wife is hesitant to be submissive, I must ask myself if I am failing to consider her interests above my own or failing to communicate how I am seeking to care for her interests above my own. A resistance to being led usually reveals a deficiency in my Christ-like leadership. Constrained submission is not Ephesians 5. Christ-like leadership and "Lord Business" have nothing in common. Selfish husbands with kicking and screaming wives do not resemble the restorative order Paul envisions here.

Human marriage opens up a window for the world to behold the beauty of the mystery. That is why Paul follows God's original blueprint for marriage - "For this reason a man will leave his father and mother and be joined to his wife, and the two will become one flesh" - with this statement: "This mystery is profound, but I am talking about Christ and the church" (Ephesians 5:32). A man and woman who unite in marriage translate the unifying dynamic of the mystery, the two becoming one, from theory into reality. Marriage displays the mystery. Sacrificial husbands and submissive wives woo people to God's wisdom at work in the mystery.

Submission in the Family

Paul then transitions from marriage to the family in Ephesians 6:1-4. When families embody this "otherworldly" submissiveness, they become a compelling demonstration of the gospel's power. They declare that the Repairman is open for business to mend our brokenness.

After I tell people that I meet that I have four kids, I usually don't have to wait very long for their jaws to drops and for this question to be asked, "How do you do that?" or some people go so far to say, "What were you thinking?" Everyone with kids knows family life is hard. The world sees kids as more of a burden than a blessing. But that is evidence we keep going to the wrong repairman to fix what is broken. Family life can be different. Kids can get along with their parents and parents can lovingly train their kids. It is possible. It requires intentionality, but it is possible by God's grace.

An orderly, submissive home is only made possible by the Spirit who empowers this new community to embrace God's design (Ephesians 5:18-21). Paul's instruction to families in Ephesians 6:1-3 still lies in the shadows of 5:18-21 where he encourages the church to be filled with the Spirit. Familial relationships are rearranged by the Spirit's presence. Children become submissive. Parents forsake forms of authority that oppress their children for ones that nurture them. The toxic environment of oppressive discipline and opposition to authority is exchanged for the health of love and respect.

Paul shows how the Spirit produces this posture of submissiveness toward their parents in children:

> "Children, obey your parents as you would the Lord, because this is right. Honor your father and mother, which is the first commandment with a promise, so that it may go well with you and that you may have a long life in the land" (Ephesians 6:1-3).

Notice that children are to obey their parents as *they would the Lord*. Reverence for Christ permeates all of life. It is not segmented to the public or the private realm, the religious or the secular. Christ is Lord of all, thus He transforms all and the Spirit's presence keeps us mindful of Christ's supremacy.

There are two incentives for this submissive spirit. The first is that obedience to parents is right (6:1b). God's command to honor the family structure has not been rescinded; it is still the way of wisdom. The second incentive inspires submission through what obedience promises. God reserved a unique blessing for those who honor this familial authority structure. It will "go well" with those who obey, which further defined, leads to a "long life in the land" (6:2-3). Children who dismiss their parents' authority end up hurting themselves. God established the family structure as a good expression of His authority. His good ways lead to life. Spirit-filled homes embrace His order.

Just like husbands have a responsibility to pave the way for submission to be easier for their wives, fathers have this responsibility with their kids. It is very important for fathers particularly to express their authority in ways that accord with how God has expressed His. Paul writes, "Fathers, don't stir up anger in your children, but bring them up in the training and instruction of the Lord" (6:4). Here, anger in children seems to result from overbearing or oppressive forms of fatherly authority. Fathers who need to enforce their authority in suppressive ways need to check themselves. Suppression does not engender the submission Paul has in view.

As a father, my kids often meet my inner "Lord Business." My "no" is often my form of the kragle. My business is controlling them and not inconveniencing myself. That is stifling to kids. I have to learn and relearn the way God exercises His authority. We can recall that God's first expression of authority in the Bible benefitted humanity. It was very good (read Genesis 1!). Children who can't sense this "good," even in discipline, are being prodded toward resentful resistance against their fathers. Fathers who provide appropriate discipline and Christ-centered instruction nurture spiritual health in their children. The winsomeness of God's wisdom showcases itself. They realize God's wisdom isn't limiting their joy but expanding it. Instead of provoking their children to anger, Spirit-filled fathers promote submissiveness. Heavy-handed fathers, on the other hand, drive their children away from themselves and away from the Lord.

Submission at Work

Paul moves beyond the family to work relationships in Ephesians 6:5-9. Work was also harmfully affected by the first sin of man. It is no secret that the frustrations associated with work abound. Long hours, overbearing bosses, lazy employees, exhausting labors – it is all there. This is the fruit of the tragic choice to forsake the restful provision God provided in Eden. Work is indeed *hard* work.

Work is still hard for the people Christ is re-creating, but there is a new way. A new story unfolding. All of life now drips with Christ's fullness. His sovereignty knows no limits. Notice this Christ-oriented slant to every aspect of a slave's relationship to his master:

> "Slaves, obey your human masters with fear and trembling, in the sincerity of your heart, as to Christ. Don't work only while being watched, in order to please men, but as slaves of Christ, do God's will from your heart. Serve with a good attitude, as to the Lord and not to men, knowing that whatever good each one does, slave or free, he will receive this back from the Lord. And masters, treat your slaves the same way, without threatening them, because you know that both their Master and yours is in heaven, and there is no favoritism with Him" (Ephesians 6:5-9).

Here is the point: work is not merely about work. It's not about masters and slaves, and it's not about wages and hours. What is it about? Christ. Christian employers and employees must see beyond the business and the busyness to Christ. Work becomes an avenue to display the glory of Christ through the manner in which they work ("good attitude"), the quality of their work ("good"), and the sincerity of their approach to work ("from the heart," "as to Christ"). The Master in heaven establishes the "payday" that surpasses all earthly paydays. Employers treat employees with the dignity and respect that is due them, knowing that Christ rules and rewards them both. Employees work hard for their employers as if Christ employs them.

Magnifying Christ infuses the daily grind with new life and potential. It becomes an avenue for glory. This Spirit-empowered, submissive way of life looks odd to the world. Because it is. It is part of the new rebellion.

May the world see that Christ is no Lord Business through our joyful resignation to His plan. May they get a glimpse of the expansive joy of forsaking resistance to the Lord Christ. A window is opened into the new world God is recreating through the mystery through submissiveness and godly authority in the rhythms and routines of our everyday lives.

CHAPTER 19

A New Way to War

Ephesians 6:10-20

As you read Ephesians, the growing sense that your life is being enveloped by a much larger story begins settling in. This short letter to the Ephesians is not a textbook designed to merely transfer facts to us. It opens a new world in which we are to live. It unveils the story in which we find ourselves – a story of love and of war.

Love and war are two threads that weave themselves throughout these six chapters. A marriage and a battle form the backdrop for the drama of this letter. Christ is the Husband who loves extravagantly, and He is the Victor whose triumph knows no end. The cosmos sets the stage for these interwoven narrative threads. God's mystery presses these themes to their climax in Christ. The loved and the Lover will enter into the fullness of their union. The Conqueror will finish His conquest and bring His kingdom to fill heaven and earth.

It is the theme of war that gets the final focus of the letter. The church still finds herself in a battle. Paul begins this concluding section with the word "finally" in 6:10. Christ has triumphed, but the church remains in the theater of battle where His conquest has yet to be completed. The Victor has been crowned, but the war continues until the appointed time. It is "soon," but it's not finished yet (Romans 16:20). So Paul concludes the bulk of the content of the letter in this way:

> "Finally, be strengthened by the Lord and by His vast strength. Put on the full armor of God so that you can stand against the tactics of the Devil. For our battle is not against flesh and blood, but against the rulers, against the authorities, against the world powers of this darkness, against the spiritual forces of evil in the heavens. This is why you must take up the full armor of God, so that you may be able to resist in the evil day, and having prepared everything, to take your stand. Stand, therefore, with truth like a belt around your waist, righteousness like armor on your chest, and your feet sandaled with readiness for the gospel of peace.
>
> In every situation take the shield of faith, and with it you will be able to extinguish all the flaming arrows of the evil one. Take the helmet of salvation, and the sword of the Spirit, which is God's word. Pray at all times in the Spirit with every prayer and request, and stay alert in this with all perseverance and intercession for all the saints. Pray also for me, that the message may be given to me when I open my mouth to make known with boldness the mystery of the gospel. For this I am an ambassador in chains. Pray that I might be bold enough in Him to speak as I should" (Ephesians 6:10-20).

What is the church's need in this final hour? Strength and endurance. After all Paul's letter could be a little unsettling. The church at Ephesus may feel vulnerable. Paul has told her that heavenly authorities oppose her, darkness surrounds her, worldliness threatens her, and evil days await her. The devil himself watches the church, ready to pounce at the opportune time

(Ephesians 2:1-3, 3:10, 4:27, 5:6-16, 6:13). Let's face it; it seems like the odds are not in her favor.

Or are they?

In and of herself, the church is no match. These forces are beyond the church's inherent strength to overcome. They are not conquerable in our own strength in that their powers extend beyond "flesh and blood" (6:12). But these evil forces have met their match. They are under the dominion of One whose strength has proven too much for them. This is the confident tone of Paul's closing remarks. This passage sends in the reinforcements of faith the church needs to be strong until the end. The church is not mere flesh and blood either. She stands strong in the Victor, Jesus Christ.

Notice that it is the church's ability, not vulnerability, that exudes from this section (emphasis mine):

- "Put on the full armor of God so that *you can* stand against the tactics of the Devil" (6:11).

- "This is why you must take up the full armor of God, so that *you may be able* to resist in the evil day, and having prepared everything, to take your stand" (6:13).

- "In every situation take the shield of faith, and with it *you will be able* to extinguish all the flaming arrows of the evil one" (6:16).

Courage in Christ, not cowardice, opens the path to realizing the victory that is hers in Him. She has every reason to be courageous for she is able to endure the attacks of the evil one. Why? Ephesians 6:10 gives the answer: "Be strengthened by the Lord and by His vast strength." In Christ, the church is able. His strength is all the reinforcements she needs. Christ's vast strength breeds confidence. The war may not be over, but in Him the battle lines can hold. She is safe in His hands.

Most battles involve taking ground from our enemies or driving them to retreat and eventual defeat. This simply is not needed in this battle. The enemy's ground has been taken. He operates on borrowed time. This makes for a strange war and an odd method of battle. The only thing needed to secure the church's triumph is captured in this one word: stand. "Stand, therefore, with truth like a belt around your waist, righteousness like armor on your chest, and your feet sandaled with readiness for the gospel of peace" (6:14-15). The church can stand strong in battle because God seated Christ far above all authority and put all things under His feet. There is no need for her to win new ground. Christ has won. She simply needs to stand in His victory.

But how exactly does the church stand in Him? Verse 11 connects this "standing" with armor: "Put on the full armor of God so that you can stand against the tactics of the Devil" (6:11). Standing against Satan results from being clothed in God's armor. What is it about this armor that withstands the onslaught of the devil himself? Its impenetrable strength stems from its Owner. It is the armor of God, particularly of His Victor, Christ.

Many commentators and preachers take us back to the Roman army as the background through which we must understand this armor. There may be something to learn there, but largely I think this approach misses the point. Most of the armor pieces that Paul mentions are images drawn from the Old Testament, particularly from the book of Isaiah (emphasis added):

"He put on righteousness like a *breastplate*, and a *helmet of salvation* on His head; He put on garments of vengeance for clothing, and He wrapped Himself in zeal as in a cloak" (Isaiah 59:17).
"Righteousness will be a *belt* around His loins; *faithfulness* will be a belt around His waist" (Isaiah 11:5).

"How beautiful on the mountains are the *feet* of the herald, who proclaims *peace*, who brings news of good things, who proclaims salvation, who says to Zion, 'Your God reigns!'" (Isaiah 52:7)

Notice that it is the messengers who carry good news of peace who have the beautiful feet in Isaiah 52. They announce that God has accomplished the victory. The victory and sovereignty are His! Zooming back and looking at the big picture of the book of Isaiah, who is the Warrior through whom God won? The Messiah. God clothed the Messiah with His own armor to go into battle. He wore the breastplate of righteousness and the belt of truth. He wore the helmet of salvation. He wore that armor and won. The Messiah, clothed in God's armor, triumphed over His foes and received the spoils of victory (Isaiah 53:12).

Why does Paul want the church to stand in armor that's already been used by the Messiah? Because of its proven worth. Because Christ secures her share in His victory. Because in Him she wins.

This armor expresses our union with Christ. Withstanding the devil is possible for us precisely because we are not clothed in our own armor but in the very armor of Christ. In union with Him, we wear His battle-worn armor and win. We stand in Him, and we are safe.

But there is more to this strange way of warring. Paul continues, "In every situation take the shield of faith, and with it you will be able to extinguish all the flaming arrows of the evil one. Take the helmet of salvation, and the sword of the Spirit, which is God's Word" (6:16-17). It is not more concerted effort that secures the victory. Paul's not rallying the troops to get them to try harder. The way forward is simple faith.

Faith extinguishes the fiery darts of accusations and unbelief that the evil one throws at the church. It may be a different "gospel," it may be a distorted "gospel," it may be no "gospel" at all. These darts are intended to move believers away from bold hope in their union with Christ to some counterfeit substitute for Christ. Faith silences the enemy's accusations that Christ is not good enough. Faith sees no need to add to Christ's sufficiency. Faith looks beyond the seen to the unseen. Faith stands in Christ alone. Faith forms a shield around us.

This faith receives its power to protect from the Word of God: "Every word of God proves true, He is a shield to those who take refuge in Him" (Proverbs 30:5 NASU). Paul seems to be tracking with Proverbs 30 as also links God's protective power with His proven Word: "Take the helmet of salvation and the sword of the Spirit, which is God's Word." The Word of God fuels and fortifies the faith that nullifies the assaults of the devil. The evil one retreats from the mighty sword of the Spirit. The reliability of God's promises protect us in battle. Satan cannot shake us when we are surrounded by God's promises that are ours in Christ.

My family tries to read *The Pilgrim's Progress* together at least once a year. One scene particularly unsettled the kids last year - the dark scene when Christian meets Beezlebub, representing the devil, for that epic battle. When Christian first beheld its ghastly figure along the path, his first response was flight. But he cannot run because he realizes his armor does not cover his back. Christian puts up a valiant effort, but Beezlebub proves to be too much for most of the fight. Christian is pinned down, on the verge of meeting his end, when he pulls out a dagger from Micah Chapter 7 that sends the dragon fleeing: "Do not rejoice over me, my enemy! Though I have fallen, I will rise!" That blow proved too much for the devil. Beezlebub never reappears on Christian's journey to the heavenly city.

John Bunyan, the author of *The Pilgrim's Progress*, knew Ephesians. The sword of the Spirit which is the Word of God sends the devil scrambling. Faith in Christ proves too strong to overcome. The devil can forget rejoicing over the church. She may fall, but she will rise.

Paul concludes this section and the letter itself with a blitzing emphasis on prayer: "Pray at all times in the Spirit with every prayer and request, and stay alert in this with all perseverance and intercession for all the saints" (Ephesians 6:18). He mentions prayer or praying four times in this one verse in the original language, and the main verb to pray is not a command in the original either. This verse flows from the previous section. In other words, it is not a new command. The point? Taking up the full armor and standing firm happens through prayer. Praying in the Spirit fits the armor to us and us to the armor of Christ. A prayerless warrior stands vulnerable. Through faith-filled prayer, we are protected and preserved.

Satan must be the most frustrated enemy ever. I think I may have felt a little bit of his frustration back in college. I went to NC State, and my soon wife-to-be girlfriend went to UNC-Chapel Hill. NC State fans hate UNC athletics with a passion. But the problem is, the hatred isn't reciprocated as strongly. UNC fans hate Duke athletics. Duke is their main rival, not State. I would go to games with her and wear my State red and the UNC fans wouldn't heckle me at all. But the minute Bec showed up in Carolina blue to a State game, she was in for it. I was so frustrated. I could not get them to fight with me because they were focused elsewhere. It used to bother me until I just stopped fighting it. It wasn't worth the effort.

Satan must be fuming as well. He wants the church to turn her focus to him, but she keeps her focus on Christ. He wants her to wrestle with him but what does she do? She wrestles in prayer. Her focus is fixed on Christ as she engages Him on her knees. Praying and pleading, the devil cannot touch her. Maybe he flees not merely because his attempts to ruin her are frustrated at every turn but also because he is so frustrated with her way of fighting.

It's a whole new way to war.

Praying for the Front Lines

Paul concludes this blitzing emphasis on prayer with a personal request. Verse 19 literally begins "and for me," which ties it to the previous context of spiritual warfare and prayer. Praying for Paul is engagement in war. Christ's conquest is not yet complete, and Paul is a soldier. He is the bearer of the good news that Christ has won. His feet are sandaled with "readiness for the gospel of peace" (6:15). What does Paul need in order to be a faithful as a good soldier? He outlines his needs in verses 19-20:

> "Pray also for me, that the message may be given to me when I open my mouth to make known with boldness the mystery of the gospel. For this I am an ambassador in chains. Pray that I might be bold enough in Him to speak as I should" (Ephesians 6:19-20).

It is texts like these that helped John Piper liken prayer to a "wartime walkie-talkie."[38] Here is Piper's full quote: "The number one reason why prayer malfunctions in the hands of a believers is that they try to turn a wartime walkie-talkie into a domestic intercom." Wartime walkie-talkies are used for the advance of the mission. Prayer is not merely about us staying safe in the battle. It is about bringing others in to be safe as well.

Paul ends the core of this letter with an invitation. It is an invitation to engage in the battle through prayerfully advancing the cause. God's reconciling mystery isn't finished reconciling. Christ's victory hasn't yet been heralded to all the nations. More than 7,000 people groups have yet to be clued in to God's plan in Christ as of 2015. Paul set his sights on those who have yet to hear. He wants the world to know the veil has been removed. The church is God's vehicle to take that news to the nations through its corporate witness to the mystery and its prayerful support of the frontline troops.

---

[38] John Piper, http://www.desiringgod.org/conference-messages/prayer-the-work-of-missions.

Through Ephesians, we are invited into this active, prayerful advance of God's mystery. Paul hands us a wartime walkie-talkie for a peace-making mission.

What should we pray for to advance the cause of the gospel? This is how Paul outlines his need in verses 19-20: clarity in proclamation and boldness to proclaim. He does not request prayer for freedom from his chains but freedom in speech for the sake of the gospel! Paul's request of the Ephesians is echoed by the Christians who live among the unreached today. It is boldness they need. It is the advance of the gospel they desire. The unfolding of the mystery consumes them. They have tasted life beyond the veil and have found the riches of God's grace sufficient for their every need. They have begun to witness their sad divisions cease and it thrills them with the possibilities of what could be. The unveiled mystery has unleashed them into the world that needs the good news.

It's the good news of grace – for us, for the nations - that waits just beyond the veil.

CONCLUSION

Ernest Gordon, a soldier in the 93rd Highlanders Division of Scotland in the Second World War, witnessed the miracle of the mystery unveiled firsthand. He recounts his experiences in his book entitled *To End to All Wars*. He and thousands of other prisoners of war were held captive in a camp in Southeast Asia. The Japanese army slavishly employed them to finish the Burma railway and build a bridge over the Kwai River. In the midst of construction, unbeknownst to them, God was building another bridge.

They suffered much at the hands of their Japanese captors. Beyond that, malaria, dysentery, and death were their constant companions. Every man's aim became simply to survive. Gordon noted that the "atmosphere became poisoned" as the governing ethic became "I look out for myself and to hell with everyone else."[39] Even the lame and dying were treated harshly for not doing their part and leaving their share to others.

Then the veil was lifted. A transformation among the community of captors began when three Christian prisoners started serving Gordon and the other men instead of merely looking out for their own interests. One stepped in to take the blame for a crime he didn't commit so that more lives would not be lost. One so tirelessly served his comrade that he collapsed and died.

---

[39] Gordon, Ernest, Location *To End All Wars,* Zondervan, 1963. Epub edition February 2014. 1131, 1252.

In the wake of such selfless love, the camp was abuzz with how Christ too had laid down His life so that others might live. This enabled them to see beyond themselves and beyond the veil. Prisoners who were fighting each other to survive began fighting so that others might live. The atmosphere had changed from one of poison to peace. Death still surrounded them but it "no longer had the last word."[40] Gordon reflected, "God, in finding us, had enabled us to find our brother."[41] A bridge had opened through the cross to be reconciled to God and to each other. The mystery was unleashed among them.

Over three years after Gordon arrived at the camp, the war finally ended with the Allied forces triumphing. As the victors marched in on the Japanese war camps, they were astounded by the conditions they saw and "were ready to kill the Japanese on the spot." But the miracle continued. The prisoners stopped them. "Captors were spared by their captives. 'Let mercy take the place of bloodshed,' said these exhausted but forgiving men," Gordon recollected.[42]

Mercy over vengeance, unity over division, peace over war - those prisoners knew the power of the cross. They witnessed the unfolding of the mystery. They knew the grace beyond the veil.

> "O come, Desire of nations, bind
> In one the hearts of all mankind;
> Oh, bid our sad divisions cease,
> And be Yourself our King of peace."[43]

Amen.

---

[40] Gordon, Ernest, Location 1739.

[41] Gordon, Ernest, Location 3306.

[42] Gordon, Ernest, Location 3411.

[43] "O Come O Come Emmanuel" A Hymn Translated by John Neal.

BIBLIOGRAPHY

Alcorn, Randy. *The Treasure Principle, Multnomah Books, 2001.*

Cowper, William. "God Moves in a Mysterious Way," Quoted in *Twenty-six Letters on Religious Subjects* by John Newton, 1774.

Crossman Samuel. "My Song Is Love Unknown," 1664.

Dever, Mark. Sermon delivered during the 2009 Bethlehem Pastor's Conference in Minneapolis, Minnesota.

Edwards, Jonathan. *Charity and Its Fruits,* The Banner of Truth Trust, 2005.

Fee, Gordon. *God's Empowering Presence*, Baker Academic Press, 2009.

Gordon, Ernest. *To End All Wars,* Zondervan, First published by Wm Collins Sons & Co. under the title *Through the Valley of the Kwai* and in 1965 by Fontana/Fount Paperbacks under the title *Miracle on the River Kwai.* Epub 2014.

Harvey, Dave. *When Sinners Say I Do: Recovering the Power of the Gospel for Marriage,*

Holman Christian Standard Bible. Holman Bible Publishers. 2009.

Keller, Timothy and Kathy. "Gospel Re-enacment: Cultivating a Healthy Marriage" Teaching given on April 1, 2005 at Redeemer Presbyterian Church.

Leeman, Jonathan. *Reverberation: How God's Word Brings Light, Freedom, and Action to His People,* Moody Publishing Company, 2011.

Lovelace, Richard. *Renewal as a Way of Life: A Guidebook for the Spiritual Life,* Wipf and Stock Publishers, 2002.

Luther, Martin. "A Mighty Fortress is Our God," Written in 1529.Translated into English by Frederick Hedge, 1853.

Macarthur, John. A Sermon on Sanctification delivered at the 2001 Shepherd's Conference.

Neal, John. Translated "O Come O Come Emmanuel" From the Lutheran Hymnal First Published in 1854.

New American Standard Version of the Bible Updated, The Lockman Foundation, 2003.

Ortlund, Ray. The Gospel Coalition Blog, Posted on November 18, 2012.

Osborne, Larry. *Sticky Teams: Keeping Your Leadership Team and Staff on the Same Page,* Zondervan, 2011.

Parnell, Jonathan. "What Our Anger Is Telling Us," published at www.desiringgod.org/blog on May 22, 2014.

Piper, John. http://www.desiringgod.org/conference-messages/prayer-the-work-of-missions Plantinga, Cornelius. *Not the Way It's Supposed to Be: A Breviary of Sin,* Wm. B. Eerdmans Publishing Co., 1995.

Spurgeon, Charles. "Best Donation," a sermon delivered on April 5, 1891 at the Metropolitan Tabernacle in London, England.

Tozer, A. W. *The Pursuit of God*, A WLC Book.

Wells, David. 2006 Desiring God National Conference Preview Video.

Wells, David. *Losing Our Virtue: Why the Church Must Recover Its Moral Vision*, William B. Eerdmans Publishing Co., 1998.

Wells, David. *No Place for Truth*, William B. Eerdmans Publishing Co., 1993.

Wesley, Charles. "And Can It Be?" from *Psalms and Hymns*, 1738.

Wilson, Doug. Blog and Mablog, Hebrews 3 Meditation, Date Unknown. Wilson, Doug. Blog Post "Is Christianity Good for the World?" on Christianity Today, June 1, 2007.

Winfrey, Oprah. "Oprah's Guide to Authentic Power," from http://www.oprahmag.co.za/live-your-best-life/self development/oprah%E2%80%99s-guide-to-authentic-power. Posted October 2013.

Wurmbrand, Richard. *In God's Underground*, Kindle Edition. Living Sacrifice Book Company, 2011.

Made in the USA
Columbia, SC
24 August 2022

65981209R00117